At Sylvan, we believe that everyone can master math skills, and we are glad you have chosen our resources to help your children experience the joy of mathematics as they build crucial reasoning skills. We know that time spent reinforcing lessons learned in school will contribute to understanding and mastery.

Success in math requires more than just memorizing basic facts and algorithms; it also requires children to make connections between the real world and math concepts in order to solve problems. Successful problem solvers will be ready for the challenges of mathematics as they advance to more complex topics and encounter new problems both in school and at home.

We use a research-based, step-by-step process in teaching math at Sylvan that includes thought-provoking math problems and activities. As students increase their success as problem solvers, they become more confident. With increasing confidence, students build even more success. The design of the Sylvan workbooks lays out a roadmap for mathematical learning that is designed to lead your child to success in school.

Included with your purchase of this workbook is a coupon for a discount at a participating Sylvan center. We hope you will use this coupon to further your children's academic journeys. Let us partner with you to support the development of confident, well-prepared, independent learners.

The Sylvan Team

Sylvan Learning Center
Unleash your child's potential here

No matter how big or small the academic challenge, every child has the ability to learn. But sometimes children need help making it happen. Sylvan believes every child has the potential to do great things. And, we know better than anyone else how to tap into that academic potential so that a child's future really is full of possibilities. Sylvan Learning Center is the place where your child can build and master the learning skills needed to succeed and unlock the potential you know is there.

The proven, personalized approach of our in-center programs deliver unparalleled results that other supplemental education services simply can't match. Your child's achievements will be seen not only in test scores and report cards but outside the classroom as well. And when he starts achieving his full potential, everyone will know it. You will see a new level of confidence come through in everything he does and every interaction he has.

How can Sylvan's personalized in-center approach help your child unleash his potential?

• Starting with our exclusive Sylvan Skills Assessment®, we pinpoint your child's exact academic needs.

• Then we develop a customized learning plan designed to achieve your child's academic goals.

• Through our method of skill mastery, your child will not only learn and master every skill in his personalized plan, he will be truly motivated and inspired to achieve his full potential.

To get started, included with this Sylvan product purchase is $10 off our exclusive Sylvan Skills Assessment®. Simply use this coupon and contact your local Sylvan Learning Center to set up your appointment.

And to learn more about Sylvan and our innovative in-center programs, call 1-800-EDUCATE or visit www.SylvanLearning.com. *With over 1,000 locations in North America, there is a Sylvan Learning Center near you!*

3rd Grade
Basic Math Success

Published in the United States by Random House, Inc., New York, and in Canada by Random House of
Canada Limited, Toronto.

www.tutoring.sylvanlearning.com

Created by Smarterville Productions LLC
Producer & Editorial Direction: The Linguistic Edge
Producer: TJ Trochlil McGreevy
Writer: Amy Kraft
Cover and Interior Illustrations: Shawn Finley and Duendes del Sur
Layout and Art Direction: SunDried Penguin
Director of Product Development: Russell Ginns

First Edition

ISBN: 978-0-375-43039-8

Library of Congress Cataloging-in-Publication Data available upon request.

This book is available at special discounts for bulk purchases for sales promotions or premiums.
For more information, write to Special Markets/Premium Sales, 1745 Broadway, MD 6-2,
New York, New York 10019 or e-mail specialmarkets@randomhouse.com.

PRINTED IN CHINA

10 9 8 7 6 5 4 3 2 1

Contents

Contents

Find Your Place

IDENTIFY the place of each digit. Then WRITE the digit.

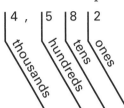

Commas make numbers easier to read. A comma belongs after the thousands place.

Example:

9,214

ones	4
tens	1
hundreds	2
thousands	9

1. **1,805**

ones _____

tens _____

hundreds _____

thousands _____

2. **7,336**

ones _____

tens _____

hundreds _____

thousands _____

3. **8,240**

ones _____

tens _____

hundreds _____

thousands _____

4. **3,699**

ones _____

tens _____

hundreds _____

thousands _____

5. **6,002**

ones _____

tens _____

hundreds _____

thousands _____

6. **2,173**

ones _____

tens _____

hundreds _____

thousands _____

Place Value

Number Words

WRITE the number words.

HINT: A comma goes after the thousands in the written form of the number, just like in the number itself.

Example: 8,172   8,172 in written form is
eight thousand, one hundred seventy-two.

1. 6,405   six thousand, four hundred five

2. 1,538   _____

3. 2,780   _____

4. 4,999   _____

5. 7,263   _____

6. 9,314   _____

WRITE the number.

7. three thousand, five hundred seventy-six   3,576

8. eight thousand, six hundred thirty-three   _____

9. five thousand, two hundred ten   _____

10. nine thousand, eight hundred ninety-one   _____

11. seven thousand, three hundred forty-five   _____

12. one thousand, four hundred fifty-two   _____

Get in Place

WRITE how many thousands, hundreds, tens, and ones you see. Then WRITE the number.

1.
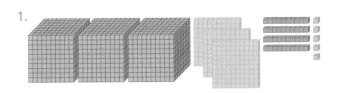

Thousands	Hundreds	Tens	Ones

=

_____

2.
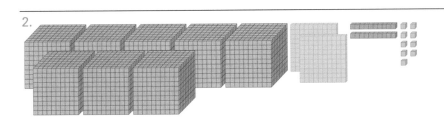

Thousands	Hundreds	Tens	Ones

=

_____

3.
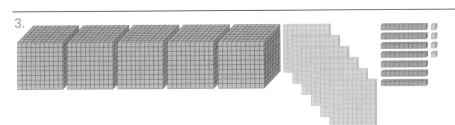

Thousands	Hundreds	Tens	Ones

=

_____

4.
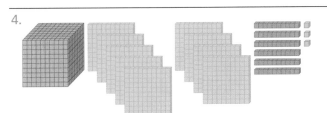

Thousands	Hundreds	Tens	Ones

=

_____

5.
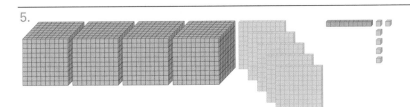

Thousands	Hundreds	Tens	Ones

=

_____

6.

Thousands	Hundreds	Tens	Ones

=

_____

Place Value

Money's Worth

WRITE how much money you see in each picture.

$1,000 $100 $10 $1

1.

$ _____ , _____

2.

$ _____ , _____

3.

$ _____ , _____

4.

$ _____ , _____

5.

$ _____ , _____

6.

$ _____ , _____

Mismatched

WRITE > or < in each box.

650 < 825
1

503 > 490 ✓
2

239 > 223 ✓
3

2,879 < 4,923 ✓
4

6,067 < 8,489 ✓
5

7,445 > 6,301 ✓
6

5,636 > 5,207 ✓
7

2,389 < 3,289 ✓
8

9,591 < 9,958 ✓
9

6,892 > 6,799 ✓
10

3,140 < 3,410 ✓
11

1,655 > 1,556 ✓
12

9,008 > 9,001 ✓
13

4,128 < 4,182 ✓
14

3,372 < 3,374 ✓
15

100%

12/12

Comparing Numbers

Matched or Mismatched?

WRITE >, <, or = in each box.

1. $3,822 ☐

2. $2,569 ☐

3. $5,282 ☐

4. $9,177 ☐

5. $6,408 ☐

6. $7,325 ☐

2

Which One?

CIRCLE the largest number in each row.

1. 4,285   1,290   3,534   (6,672)

2. (9,158)   6,923   7,227   8,831

3. 5,746   (4,955)   (5,803)   5,069

4. 4,890   4,385   4,761   (4,910)

5. (7,398)   7,374   7,212   7,356

6. 3,841   (3,848)   3,840   3,835

Which One?

CIRCLE the smallest number in each row.

1. 5,208   (4,763)   8,459   5,530

2. (7,848)   8,125   7,957   (8,002)

3. (3,491)   4,862   (3,399)   (4,153)

4. 6,589   (6,332)   6,912   6,474

5. 2,174   (2,238)   (2,634)   (2,165)

6. 9,530   (9,602)   ~~9,592~~   (9,528)

Round About

Rounding makes numbers easier to work with.

Numbers that end in 1 through 4 get rounded **down** to the nearest ten.

Numbers that end in 5 through 9 get rounded **up** to the nearest ten.

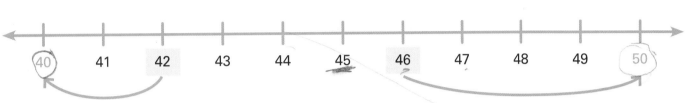

Numbers that end in 1 through 49 get rounded **down** to the nearest hundred.

Numbers that end in 50 through 99 get rounded **up** to the nearest hundred.

ROUND each number to the nearest ten.

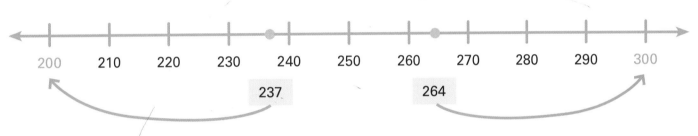

1. 22 __20__   2. 87 __90__   3. 41 __40__   4. 94 __90__
5. 53 __50__   6. 78 __80__   7. 16 __20__   8. 35 __40__

12 __10__   65 __70__   51 __50__   77 __80__

ROUND each number to the nearest hundred.

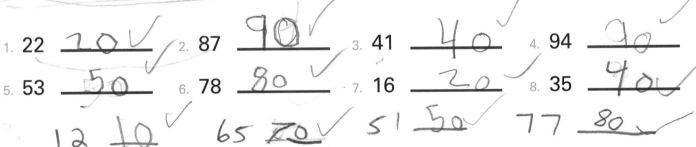

9. 504 __500__   10. 367 __400__   11. 129 __100__   12. 781 __800__
13. 472 __500__   14. 831 __800__   15. 644 __600__   16. 256 __300__

Round About

Rounding large numbers works the same way.

Numbers that end in 1 through 499 get rounded **down** to the nearest thousand.

Numbers that end in 500 through 999 get rounded **up** to the nearest thousand.

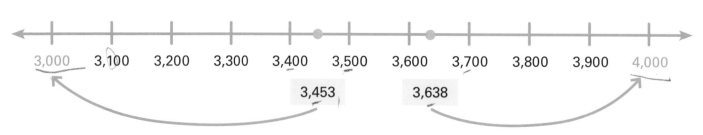

ROUND each number to the nearest thousand.

1. 7,372   7000

2. 1,239   1000

3. 5,836   6000

4. 8,199   8000

5. 2,964   3000

6. 6,078   6000

7. 8,735   9000

8. 3,484   3000

9. 1,577   2000

10. 4,179   4000

11. 7,991   8000

12. 5,639   6000

13. 3,743   4000

14. 2,804   3000

15. 6,529   7000

16. 4,495   4000

Guess and Check

Estimating is making a reasonable guess about something. ESTIMATE the amount of money in each set. Then CHECK your guess by counting the money.

1. Estimate: ──────────

   Check: ──────────

2. Estimate: ──────────

   Check: ──────────

3. Estimate: ──────────

   Check: ──────────

Loop It

ESTIMATE the number of bees. Then CIRCLE groups of 10 to count the bees and check your estimate.

Estimate: _____   Check: _____

Write the Number

WRITE the number or number words.

1. eight thousand, four hundred twenty-one — 8,421

2. three thousand, nine hundred fifty-four — 3,954

3. five thousand, seven hundred thirty-six — 5,736

4. seven thousand, six hundred seventy-seven — 7,677

5. 4,385 — four thousand three hundred eight five

6. 6,509 — six thousand five hundred and nine

7. 7,138 — seven one h seven thousand one hundred thirty eight

8. 9,870 — nine thousand eight hundred seventy

Use all of the numbers above to answer each question. WRITE the number.

9. Which number has a 1 in the ones place? — 8,421

10. Which number has an 8 in the tens place? — 4,

11. Which number has a 5 in the tens place? —

12. Which number has a 5 in the thousands place? —

13. Which number has a 3 in the hundreds place? —

14. Which number has a 9 in the thousands place? —

Unit Rewind

1. CIRCLE the largest number.

8,730   8,802   (8,810)   8,797

2. CIRCLE the smallest number.

(5,187)   5,214   5,199   5,239

ROUND each number to the nearest hundred.

672 __700__   904 __900__   853 __900__   248 __200__
     3   4   5   6

ROUND each number to the nearest thousand.

5,927 __6000__   1,256 __1000__   6,510 __7000__   3,445 __3000__
       7   8   9   10

11. ESTIMATE the number of stars. Then COUNT to check your estimate.

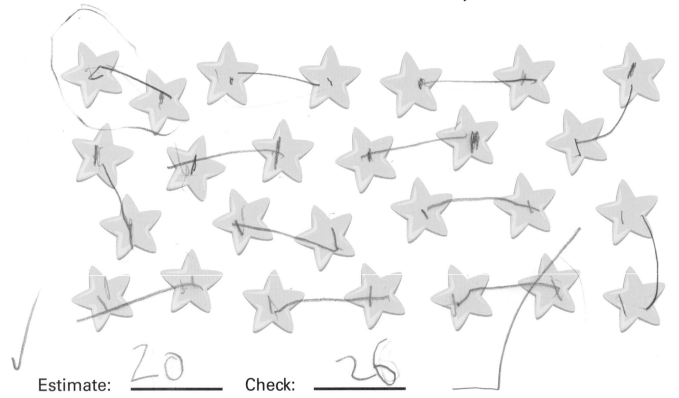

Estimate: __20__   Check: __26__

It All Adds Up

WRITE each sum.

1. 32   +   51   = _83_ ✓

2. 25   +   33   = _58_ ✓

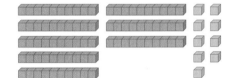

3. 89   +   10   = _99_ ✗

4. 46   +   21   = _67_ ✓

5.
```
  74
+ 13
----
  87
```
✓

6.
```
  27
+ 22
----
  49
```
✓

7.
```
  61
+ 32
----
  43
```
✓

8.
```
  23
+ 43
----
  66
```
✓

9.
```
  38
+ 21
----
  59
```
✓

10.
```
  16
+ 32
----
  48
```
✓

11.
```
  26
+ 50
----
  76
```
✓

12.
```
  71
+ 26
----
  97
```
✓

Adding & Subtracting 2-Digit Numbers

What's the Difference?

WRITE each difference.

1. 76 – 21 = _5 5_

2. 94 – 53 = _45_

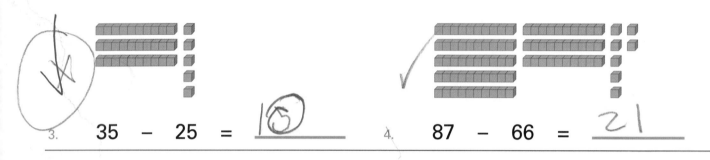

3. 35 – 25 = _10_

4. 87 – 66 = _21_

35 –
25
10

5. 88
  – 41
   47

6. 28
  – 13
   15

7. 84
  – 52
   32

8. 96
  – 43
   53

9. 79
  – 48
   31

10. 48
   – 22
    20

11. 98
   – 30
    68

12. 65
   – 53
    12

It All Adds Up

WRITE each sum.

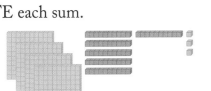

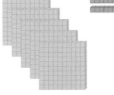

1.   463   +   126   =   _589_

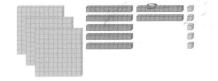

2.   370   +   524   =   _894_

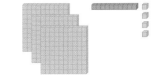
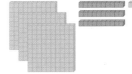

3.   314   +   244   =   _558_

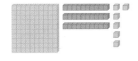
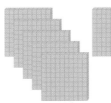

4.   136   +   331   =   _467_

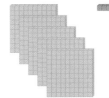

5.   375   +   602   =   _977_

6.   232   +   510   =   _742_

Adding 3-Digit Numbers

It All Adds Up

WRITE each sum.

1.
```
  415
+  32
  447
```

2.
```
  128
+  51
  179
```

3.
```
  341
+  15
  356
```

4.
```
  822
+  73
  895
```

5.
```
  656
+  43
  699
```

6.
```
  532
+  20
  552
```

7.
```
  732
+  16
  748
```

8.
```
  904
+  65
  969
```

9.
```
  231
+ 542
  773
```

10.
```
  204
+ 292
  496
```

11.
```
  824
+ 125
  949
```

12.
```
  160
+ 137
  297
```

13.
```
  451
+ 213
  664
```

14.
```
  364
+ 221
  585
```

15.
```
  191
+ 603
  794
```

16.
```
  342
+ 134
  476
```

Pick Apart

Partial sums is a method of addition, adding each place one at a time.

	6 6 4
	+ 2 5 8

Add the numbers in the hundreds place. $600 + 200 =$ 8 0 0

Add the numbers in the tens place. $60 + 50 =$ 1 1 0

Add the numbers in the ones place. $4 + 8 =$ +   1 2

Then add the numbers together.   9 2 2

WRITE each sum using partial sums.

1.
```
  516
+ 349
  865
```

2.
```
  399
+ 174
  573
```

3.
```
  472
+ 225
  697
```

4.
```
  534
+ 177
  711
```

5.
```
  290
+ 636
  926
```

6.
```
  198
+ 184
  382
```

7.
```
  427
+ 296
  723
```

8.
```
  688
+ 263
  951
```

Adding 3-Digit Numbers

It All Adds Up

WRITE each sum.

564 + 278	First, add the ones. $4 + 8 = 12$	¹ 564 + 278 2	Write a 2 in the ones place, and a 1 in the tens place. Add the tens. $1 + 6 + 7 = 14$.	¹¹ 564 + 278 42	Write a 4 in the tens place, and a 1 in the hundreds place. Add the hundreds. $1 + 5 + 2 = 8$	¹¹ 564 + 278 842	Write an 8 in the hundreds place.

1.
726
+ 185
911

2.
348
+ 297
645

3.
198
+ 593
291

4.
460
+ 323
783

5.
173
+ 248
421

6.
176
+ 329
505

7.
655
+ 177
832

8.
256
+ 256
512

9.
803
+ 129
932

10.
452
+ 368
820

11.
457
+ 243
700

12.
369
+ 288
657

22

What's the Difference?

WRITE each difference.

$$\begin{array}{r} 473 \\ -321 \\ \hline \end{array}$$

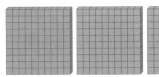

$$\begin{array}{r} 1\;5\;4 \end{array}$$

1.   473   –   321   = ___ 152

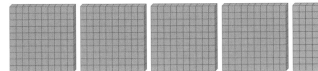

$$\begin{array}{r} 549 \\ -126 \\ \hline \end{array}$$

2.   549   –   126   = ___

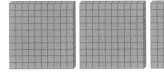

$$\begin{array}{r} 687 \\ -382 \\ \hline \end{array}$$

3.   687   –   382   = ___

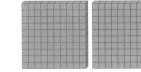

$$\begin{array}{r} 269 \\ -148 \\ \hline \end{array}$$

4.   269   –   148   = ___

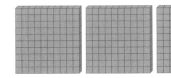

$$\begin{array}{r} 536 \\ -325 \\ \hline \end{array}$$

5.   536   –   325   = ___

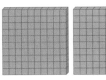

$$\begin{array}{r} 678 \\ -232 \\ \hline \end{array}$$

6.   678   –   232   = ___

Subtracting 3-Digit Numbers

What's the Difference?

WRITE each difference.

1.
```
  738
-  24
```

2.
```
  393
-  41
```

3.
```
  896
-  72
```

4.
```
  545
-  32
```

5.
```
  983
- 722
```

6.
```
  878
- 316
```

7.
```
  569
- 127
```

8.
```
  466
- 362
```

9.
```
  348
- 211
```

10.
```
  419
- 101
```

11.
```
  784
- 453
```

12.
```
  878
- 357
```

13.
```
  928
- 223
```

14.
```
  695
- 321
```

15.
```
  869
- 440
```

16.
```
  893
- 213
```

What's the Difference?

WRITE each difference.

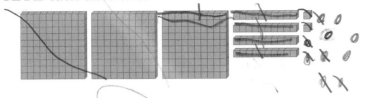

1. (342) – 158 = __184__

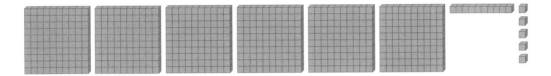

2. 615 – 407 = _____

3. 556 – 192 = _____

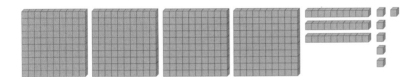

4. 436 – 288 = _____

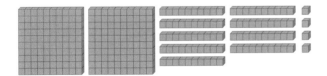

5. 294 – 235 = _____

6. 661 – 372 = _____

Subtracting 3-Digit Numbers

What's the Difference?

WRITE each difference.

5 14		5 14		7 15 14	
8̶6̶4̶	First, regroup ten from the tens place. Cross out 6 and write 5, and cross out 4 and write 14.	8̶6̶4̶	Subtract in the ones place: 14 − 7 = 7. Write 7 in the ones place.	8̶6̶4̶	Regroup from the hundreds place. Cross out 8 and write 7, and change 5 into 15. Then, subtract in the tens place: 15 − 7 = 8, and the hundreds place: 7 − 5 = 2.
− 577		− 577		− 577	
		7		287	

1.
```
   672
 − 384
```

2.
```
   720
 − 268
```

3.
```
   937
 − 241
```

4.
```
   416
 − 299
```

5.
```
   802
 − 574
```

6.
```
   671
 − 495
```

7.
```
   592
 − 347
```

8.
```
   236
 − 149
```

9.
```
   955
 − 266
```

10.
```
   834
 − 779
```

11.
```
   330
 − 182
```

12.
```
   712
 − 387
```

Trade First

With the **trade-first** method, you do the regrouping all at once. Put regrouped numbers over the "place."

	4	3	1
−	2	5	6

In the ones place, 6 cannot be subtracted from 1.

		2	11
	4	3̶	1̶
−	2	5	6

Trade 1 ten from the tens place for 10 ones, leaving 2 in the tens place and 11 in the ones place.

	3	12	11
	4̶	3̶	1̶
−	2	5	6

5 cannot be subtracted from 2, so trade 1 hundred from the hundreds place for 10 tens. This leaves a 3 in the hundreds place and 12 in the tens place.

	3	12	11
	4̶	3̶	1̶
−	2	5	6
	1	7	5

Then, subtract the numbers in every place to get the answer.

WRITE each difference using the trade-first method.

1.
```
  572
− 289
```

2.
```
  613
− 438
```

3.
```
  836
− 393
```

4.
```
  420
− 174
```

5.
```
  731
− 546
```

6.
```
  207
− 188
```

7.
```
  828
− 259
```

8.
```
  945
− 288
```

9.
```
  827
− 492
```

10.
```
  536
− 387
```

11.
```
  467
− 169
```

12.
```
  330
− 258
```

Subtracting 3-Digit Numbers

What's the Difference?

WRITE each difference.

HINT: Try using the methods of the last two pages, and decide which one works best for you.

1.
$$829 - 479$$

2.
$$740 - 272$$

3.
$$435 - 156$$

4.
$$942 - 766$$

5.
$$645 - 289$$

6.
$$511 - 388$$

7.
$$820 - 534$$

8.
$$717 - 619$$

9.
$$738 - 445$$

10.
$$927 - 490$$

11.
$$204 - 115$$

12.
$$625 - 356$$

13.
$$451 - 329$$

14.
$$872 - 185$$

15.
$$661 - 499$$

16.
$$500 - 139$$

It All Adds Up

WRITE each sum.

HINT: Add the columns starting in the ones place, the same way you would with two numbers.

Example:

```
    6 5                    1                         1
                          6 5                       6 5
    2 7                   2 7                       2 7
  + 1 3    5 + 7 + 3 = 15 + 1 3  1 + 6 + 2 + 1 = 10 + 1 3
  ─────                  ─────                     ─────
                            5                     1 0 5
```

1.
```
    7
    9
 +  4
────
```

2.
```
    6
    3
 +  8
────
```

3.
```
   12
    7
 +  6
────
```

4.
```
   35
    8
 +  7
────
```

5.
```
   46
   17
 +  6
────
```

6.
```
   90
   22
 + 73
────
```

7.
```
   56
   14
 + 66
────
```

8.
```
   41
   76
 + 26
────
```

9.
```
  187
   33
 + 29
────
```

10.
```
  432
   67
 + 14
────
```

11.
```
  520
  128
 + 73
────
```

12.
```
  426
  291
 + 83
────
```

13.
```
   76
   12
   58
 + 24
────
```

14.
```
   53
   68
   94
 + 11
────
```

15.
```
  208
  423
   50
 + 37
────
```

16.
```
  723
  109
   32
 + 95
────
```

Adding 3 or More Numbers

Pick Apart

WRITE each sum using partial sums.

Add the numbers in the hundreds place. $700 + 100 =$
Add the numbers in the tens place. $70 + 20 + 30 =$
Add the numbers in the ones place. $4 + 8 + 6 =$
Then add the numbers together.

```
  7 7 4
  1 2 8
+   3 6
  8 0 0
  1 2 0
+   1 8
  9 3 8
```

1.
```
   81
   23
+  57
```

2.
```
  464
   39
+  16
```

3.
```
  536
  182
+  72
```

4.
```
  431
  208
+ 325
```

5.
```
   64
   12
   45
+  31
```

6.
```
  671
   53
   30
+  19
```

7.
```
  325
  260
   18
+  22
```

8.
```
  124
  505
  230
+  11
```

It All Adds Up

WRITE each sum.

1.
$$5{,}234$$
$$+52$$

2.
$$3{,}716$$
$$+21$$

3.
$$9{,}348$$
$$+35$$

4.
$$7{,}724$$
$$+96$$

5.
$$6{,}409$$
$$+250$$

6.
$$4{,}131$$
$$+614$$

7.
$$1{,}259$$
$$+556$$

8.
$$3{,}517$$
$$+489$$

9.
$$1{,}294$$
$$+1{,}603$$

10.
$$3{,}371$$
$$+4{,}218$$

11.
$$4{,}102$$
$$+1{,}451$$

12.
$$4{,}525$$
$$+2{,}213$$

13.
$$2{,}385$$
$$+3{,}836$$

14.
$$1{,}680$$
$$+1{,}746$$

15.
$$2{,}831$$
$$+1{,}282$$

16.
$$8{,}057$$
$$+1{,}748$$

Adding & Subtracting 4-Digit Numbers

What's the Difference?

WRITE each difference.

1.
$$6,537 - 26$$

2.
$$1,398 - 72$$

3.
$$4,552 - 68$$

4.
$$5,117 - 44$$

5.
$$9,783 - 521$$

6.
$$7,468 - 154$$

7.
$$5,246 - 307$$

8.
$$2,287 - 295$$

9.
$$2,871 - 1,750$$

10.
$$8,599 - 3,129$$

11.
$$7,645 - 4,203$$

12.
$$9,328 - 5,211$$

13.
$$8,392 - 4,914$$

14.
$$5,042 - 2,263$$

15.
$$8,921 - 1,467$$

16.
$$6,490 - 3,581$$

Number Drop-off

Front-end estimation is a fast way to determine approximately how large a sum or difference will be.

For front-end estimation, make all but the leftmost digit of each number zero.

$$
\begin{array}{r}
6,658 \\
+\ \ \ 217 \\
\end{array}
\longrightarrow
\begin{array}{r}
6,000 \\
+\ \ \ 200 \\
\hline
6,200 \\
\end{array}
$$

6,658 becomes 6,000.
217 becomes 200.
6,000 + 200 = 6,200
6,658 + 217 = 6,875

ESTIMATE each sum using front-end estimation. Then WRITE the actual sum to see how close your estimate is to the sum.

1.
$$
\begin{array}{r}
423 \\
+\ 271 \\
\end{array}
\qquad +\ \underline{\hspace{3em}}
$$

2.
$$
\begin{array}{r}
190 \\
+\ 724 \\
\end{array}
\qquad +\ \underline{\hspace{3em}}
$$

3.
$$
\begin{array}{r}
2,385 \\
+\ \ 612 \\
\end{array}
\qquad +\ \underline{\hspace{3em}}
$$

4.
$$
\begin{array}{r}
8,732 \\
+\ \ 958 \\
\end{array}
\qquad +\ \underline{\hspace{3em}}
$$

5.
$$
\begin{array}{r}
3,361 \\
+4,518 \\
\end{array}
\qquad +\ \underline{\hspace{3em}}
$$

6.
$$
\begin{array}{r}
2,112 \\
+1,308 \\
\end{array}
\qquad +\ \underline{\hspace{3em}}
$$

Number Drop-off

ESTIMATE each difference using front-end estimation. Then WRITE the actual difference to see how close your estimate is to the difference.

For front-end estimation, make all but the leftmost digit of each number zero.

$$\begin{array}{r} 7,289 \\ -351 \\ \hline \end{array} \longrightarrow \begin{array}{r} 7,000 \\ -300 \\ \hline 6,700 \end{array}$$

7,289 becomes 7,000.
351 becomes 300.

7,000 − 300 = 6,700
7,289 − 351 = 6,938

1.
$$\begin{array}{r} 872 \\ -661 \\ \hline \end{array}$$
−_____

2.
$$\begin{array}{r} 925 \\ -629 \\ \hline \end{array}$$
−_____

3.
$$\begin{array}{r} 6,734 \\ -322 \\ \hline \end{array}$$
−_____

4.
$$\begin{array}{r} 1,283 \\ -564 \\ \hline \end{array}$$
−_____

5.
$$\begin{array}{r} 4,826 \\ -1,711 \\ \hline \end{array}$$
−_____

6.
$$\begin{array}{r} 9,382 \\ -7,449 \\ \hline \end{array}$$
−_____

Round About

Rounding numbers before adding and subtracting them often produces a closer estimate than when using front-end estimation. ROUND to the nearest hundred, and ADD the numbers to find an estimate of each sum. WRITE the sum to see how close your estimate is to the sum.

$$
\begin{array}{r}
5,1\,5\,3 \\
+\ \ \ 4\,3\,9 \\
\end{array}
\longrightarrow
\begin{array}{r}
5,2\,0\,0 \\
+\ \ \ 4\,0\,0 \\
\hline
5,6\,0\,0 \\
\end{array}
$$

5,153 rounded to the nearest hundred is 5,200.

439 rounded to the nearest hundred is 400.

5,200 + 400 = 5,600

5,153 + 439 = 5,592

1.
$$
\begin{array}{r}
436 \\
+\ 251 \\
\end{array}
\qquad
+\ \rule{3cm}{0.4pt}
$$

2.
$$
\begin{array}{r}
166 \\
+\ 108 \\
\end{array}
\qquad
+\ \rule{3cm}{0.4pt}
$$

3.
$$
\begin{array}{r}
3,524 \\
+\ \ 367 \\
\end{array}
\qquad
+\ \rule{3cm}{0.4pt}
$$

4.
$$
\begin{array}{r}
7,539 \\
+\ \ 616 \\
\end{array}
\qquad
+\ \rule{3cm}{0.4pt}
$$

5.
$$
\begin{array}{r}
2,345 \\
+2,354 \\
\end{array}
\qquad
+\ \rule{3cm}{0.4pt}
$$

6.
$$
\begin{array}{r}
4,181 \\
+1,423 \\
\end{array}
\qquad
+\ \rule{3cm}{0.4pt}
$$

Round About

ROUND to the nearest hundred, and SUBTRACT the numbers to find an estimate of each difference. WRITE the difference to see how close your estimate is to the difference.

$$
\begin{array}{r} 2,587 \\ -\ \ 534 \\ \end{array} \longrightarrow
\begin{array}{r} 2,600 \\ -\ \ 500 \\ \hline 2,100 \end{array}
$$

2,587 rounded to the nearest hundred is 2,600.
534 rounded to the nearest hundred is 500.

2,600 − 500 = 2,100
2,587 − 534 = 2,053

1.
$$
\begin{array}{r} 878 \\ -\ 223 \\ \hline \end{array}
$$
−_____

2.
$$
\begin{array}{r} 795 \\ -\ 519 \\ \hline \end{array}
$$
−_____

3.
$$
\begin{array}{r} 6,428 \\ -\ 411 \\ \hline \end{array}
$$
−_____

4.
$$
\begin{array}{r} 4,493 \\ -\ 897 \\ \hline \end{array}
$$
−_____

5.
$$
\begin{array}{r} 8,781 \\ -6,447 \\ \hline \end{array}
$$
−_____

6.
$$
\begin{array}{r} 7,064 \\ -\ 1,815 \\ \hline \end{array}
$$
−_____

Work It Out

Alex loves to collect baseball cards. He has 523 cards in his collection, and he has plans to buy 25 more cards on the weekend.

1. How many baseball cards will Alex have? _548_

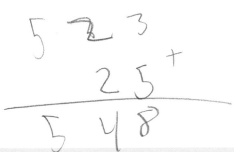

$$
\begin{array}{r}
523 \\
+\ 25 \\
\hline
548
\end{array}
$$

Pop sensation Sara O'Hara just performed two spectacular concerts. On Friday, 3,814 tickets were sold. On Saturday, 4,990 tickets were sold.

2. How many total tickets were sold? _8804_

$$
\begin{array}{r}
3814 \\
+\ 4990 \\
\hline
8804
\end{array}
$$

Alex and Jane had a lemonade stand for 4 hot days. On the first day, they sold 23 cups of lemonade. The next day, they sold 17 cups. The third day was the hottest, and they sold 42 cups. On the last day, they sold 25 cups.

3. How many total cups of lemonade did they sell? _107_

$$
\begin{array}{r}
23 \\
17\ + \\
42 \\
25 \\
\hline
\end{array}
$$

Work It Out

Mike and Marissa are on an 875-mile road trip with their parents. In three days, they traveled 526 miles.

1. How many miles do they have left to go? __349__

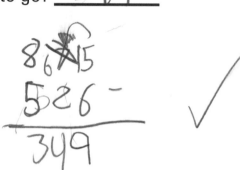

$$
\begin{array}{r}
8\,6\!\!\!/\,\cancel{7}5 \\
526\,- \\
\hline
349
\end{array}
$$

✓

Springfield Elementary School collected 1,081 cans for two soup kitchens in town. They gave 458 cans to the first soup kitchen.

2. How many cans will they give to the other soup kitchen? _____

623 ✓

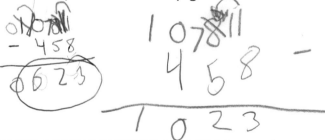

$$
\begin{array}{r}
-458 \\
\hline
\boxed{0623}
\end{array}
$$

$$
\begin{array}{r}
1\,0\,7\,8\,11 \\
4\ 5\ 8\,- \\
\hline
1\ 0\ 2\ 3
\end{array}
$$

Hannah racked up the highest score on Starship Space Race with 7,129 points. Ricky has the second-highest score with 6,832 points.

3. How many points higher is Hannah's score than Ricky's? _____

0297

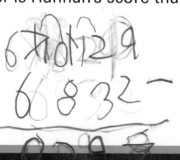

$$
\begin{array}{r}
6\,\cancel{7}\,\cancel{1}\,12\,9 \\
6\,8\,3\,2\,- \\
\hline
0297
\end{array}
$$

✓

Unit Rewind

Unit Rewind

WRITE each sum or difference.

1.
$$\begin{array}{r} 54 \\ +\ 21 \\ \hline 75 \end{array}$$

2.
$$\begin{array}{r} {}^{1}78 \\ +\ 33 \\ \hline 111 \end{array}$$

3.
$$\begin{array}{r} 86 \\ -\ 64 \\ \hline 122 \end{array}$$

4.
$$\begin{array}{r} 5\cancel{6}7 \\ -\ 28 \\ \hline 39 \end{array}$$

5.
$$\begin{array}{r} 438 \\ +\ 240 \\ \hline 678 \end{array}$$

6.
$$\begin{array}{r} {}^{11}582 \\ +\ 349 \\ \hline 931 \end{array}$$

7.
$$\begin{array}{r} 928 \\ -\ 623 \\ \hline 305 \end{array}$$

8.
$$\begin{array}{r} 3\cancel{4}\cancel{7}1 \\ -\ 177 \\ \hline 294 \end{array}$$

9.
$$\begin{array}{r} 1{,}282 \\ +\ 512 \\ \hline 1{,}794 \end{array}$$

10.
$$\begin{array}{r} {}^{111}4{,}916 \\ +\ 684 \\ \hline 5{,}600 \end{array}$$

11.
$$\begin{array}{r} 3{,}671 \\ -\ 610 \\ \hline 3{,}061 \end{array}$$

12.
$$\begin{array}{r} 7{,}102 \\ -\ 493 \\ \hline 6{,}609 \end{array}$$

13.
$$\begin{array}{r} 2{,}830 \\ +6{,}129 \\ \hline 8{,}959 \end{array}$$

14.
$$\begin{array}{r} {}^{11}3{,}817 \\ +3{,}195 \\ \hline 7{,}012 \end{array}$$

15.
$$\begin{array}{r} 9{,}844 \\ -9{,}213 \\ \hline 0{,}631 \end{array}$$

16.
$$\begin{array}{r} 4{,}164 \\ -2{,}837 \\ \hline 1{,}327 \end{array}$$

Unit Rewind

First, ESTIMATE each problem using front-end estimation. Then ESTIMATE each problem by rounding to the nearest hundred. WRITE the sum or difference to compare your estimates.

	Front End	Rounding

1.
```
    531
 +  324
```
+ _____   + _____

2.
```
  1,249
 +  217
```
+ _____   + _____

3.
```
    352
 -  144
```
- _____   - _____

4.
```
  4,671
 -  728
```
- _____   - _____

Lunch Boxes

WRITE the total number of food items you see in the four lunch boxes.

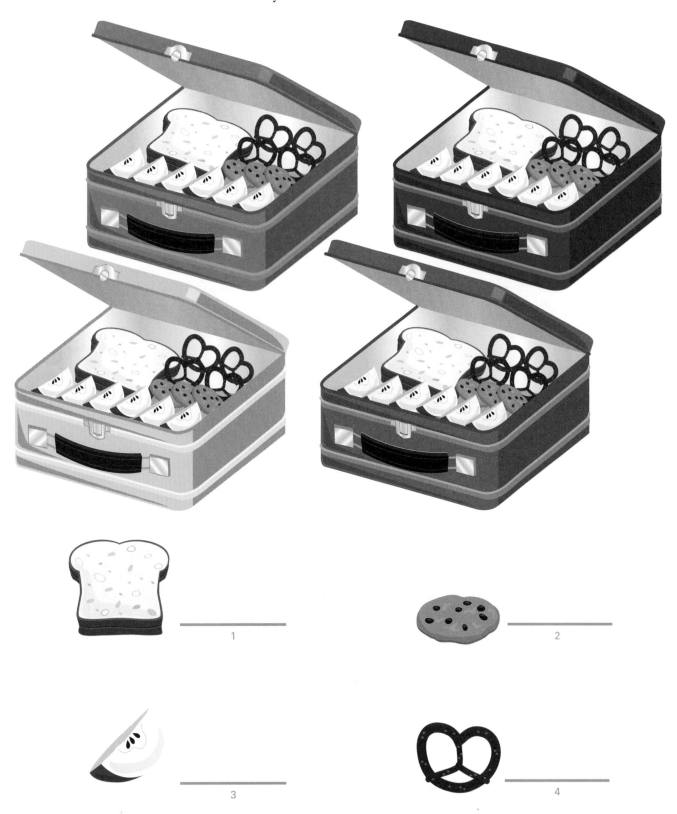

1

2

3

4

Pick a Package

How many of each type of box would be needed to pack the chocolates on the conveyor belt? WRITE the answer below each box.

1

2

3

4

Get in Line

SKIP COUNT and WRITE the missing numbers.

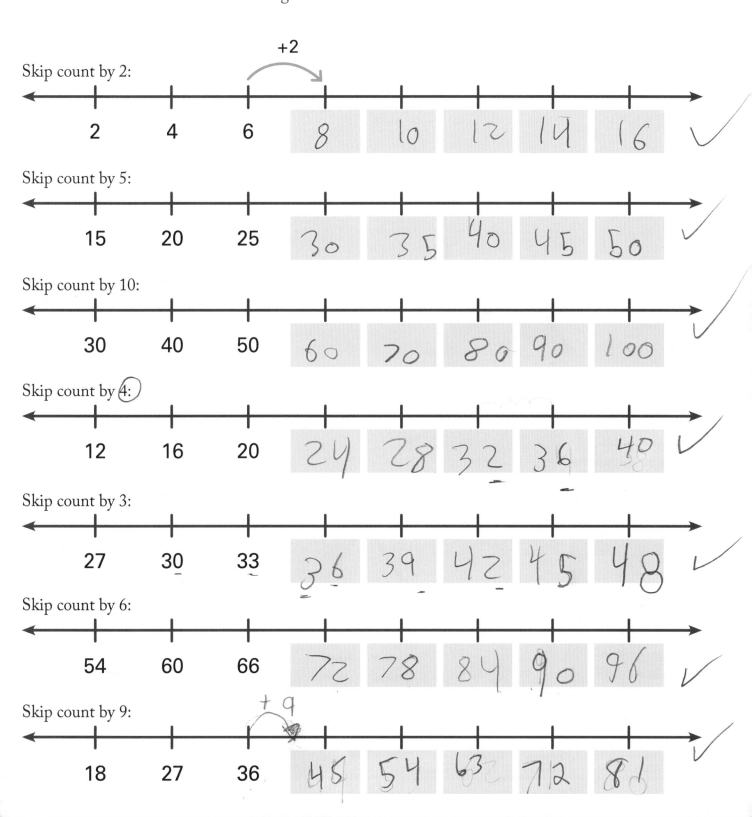

Skip count by 2:

2   4   6   8   10   12   14   16

Skip count by 5:

15   20   25   30   35   40   45   50

Skip count by 10:

30   40   50   60   70   80   90   100

Skip count by 4:

12   16   20   24   28   32   36   40

Skip count by 3:

27   30   33   36   39   42   45   48

Skip count by 6:

54   60   66   72   78   84   90   96

Skip count by 9:

18   27   36   45   54   63   72   81

Multiplying

Buildings Times Two

WRITE the number of windows you see on each building on the sign above the building.

1. $4 \times 2 = 8$
2. $6 \times 2 = 12$
3. $2 \times 2 = 4$
4. $7 \times 2 = 14$
5. $3 \times 2 = 6$

Picture It

Use the pictures to help you answer each problem. WRITE the answer for each set of pictures.

$5 \times 3 =$ _15_

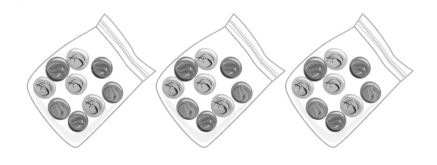

$9 \times 3 =$ _27_

$7 \times 3 =$ _21_

$6 \times 4 =$ _24_

$10 \times 4 =$ _40_

Multiplying

High Fives

Use the pictures to help you answer each problem. WRITE the answer to each problem.

HINT: Think of each problem as counting the total number of fingers on a number of hands.

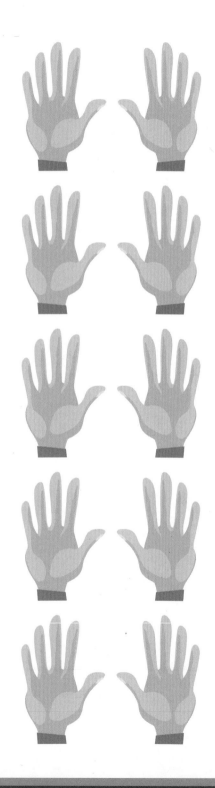

$4 \times 5 = $ ___20___
1

$1 \times 5 = $ ___5___ ✓
2

$7 \times 5 = $ ___35___ ✓
3

$6 \times 5 = $ ___30___
4

$2 \times 5 = $ ___10___ ✓
5

$9 \times 5 = $ ___45___ ✓
6

$5 \times 5 = $ ___25___ ✓
7

$8 \times 5 = $ ___40___ ✓
8

$10 \times 5 = $ ___50___ ✓
9

$3 \times 5 = $ ___15___ ✓
10

Magic Tricks

Multiplying any number by 1 gives you the same number.

Each hat has 1 rabbit.
3 hats have 3 rabbits.
3 × 1 = 3

Multiplying any number by 0 gives you 0.

Each hat has 0 rabbits.
3 hats have 0 rabbits.
3 × 0 = 0

WRITE the answer to each problem.

1.
$$
\begin{array}{r}
6 \\
\times\ 1 \\
\hline
6
\end{array}
$$

2.
$$
\begin{array}{r}
7 \\
\times\ 0 \\
\hline
0
\end{array}
$$

3.
$$
\begin{array}{r}
3 \\
\times\ 1 \\
\hline
3
\end{array}
$$

4.
$$
\begin{array}{r}
2 \\
\times\ 0 \\
\hline
0
\end{array}
$$

5.
$$
\begin{array}{r}
10 \\
\times\ 1 \\
\hline
10
\end{array}
$$

6.
$$
\begin{array}{r}
8 \\
\times\ 0 \\
\hline
0
\end{array}
$$

7.
$$
\begin{array}{r}
5 \\
\times\ 1 \\
\hline
5
\end{array}
$$

8.
$$
\begin{array}{r}
4 \\
\times\ 0 \\
\hline
0
\end{array}
$$

9.
$$
\begin{array}{r}
1 \\
\times\ 1 \\
\hline
1
\end{array}
$$

10.
$$
\begin{array}{r}
5 \\
\times\ 0 \\
\hline
0
\end{array}
$$

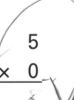

11.
$$
\begin{array}{r}
9 \\
\times\ 1 \\
\hline
9
\end{array}
$$

12.
$$
\begin{array}{r}
10 \\
\times\ 0 \\
\hline
0
\end{array}
$$

13.
$$
\begin{array}{r}
7 \\
\times\ 1 \\
\hline
7
\end{array}
$$

14.
$$
\begin{array}{r}
6 \\
\times\ 0 \\
\hline
0
\end{array}
$$

15.
$$
\begin{array}{r}
8 \\
\times\ 1 \\
\hline
8
\end{array}
$$

16.
$$
\begin{array}{r}
1 \\
\times\ 0 \\
\hline
0
\end{array}
$$

17.
$$
\begin{array}{r}
2 \\
\times\ 1 \\
\hline
2
\end{array}
$$

18.
$$
\begin{array}{r}
9 \\
\times\ 0 \\
\hline
0
\end{array}
$$

Picture It

Use the pictures to help you answer each problem. WRITE the answer for each set of pictures.

1.

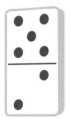 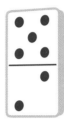 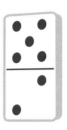 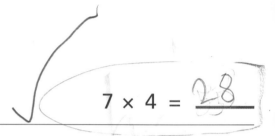

$7 \times 4 = \underline{28}$

2.

 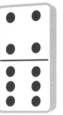 

$10 \times 3 = \underline{30}$

3.

 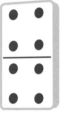 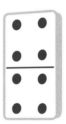 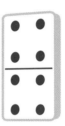  

$8 \times 6 = \underline{48}$

4.

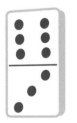 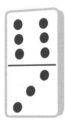 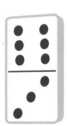 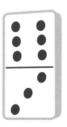

$9 \times 4 = \underline{28}$

5.

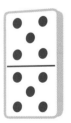 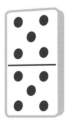 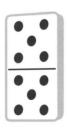 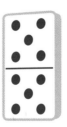 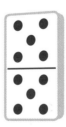 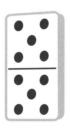 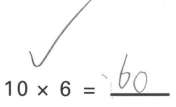

$10 \times 6 = \underline{60}$

Computation Station

A **product** is the number you get when you multiply two numbers together. A **factor** is one of the numbers being multiplied.

Example:

```
      6   factor
   ×  7   factor
     4 2  product
```

factor

factor →

×	0	1	2	3	4	5	6	7	8	9	10
0	0	0	0	0	0	0	0	0	0	0	0
1	0	1	2	3	4	5	6	7	8	9	10
2	0	2	4	6	8	10	12	14	16	18	20
3	0	3	6	9	12	15	18	21	24	27	30
4	0	4	8	12	16	20	24	28	32	36	40
5	0	5	10	15	20	25	30	35	40	45	50
6	0	6	12	18	24	30	36	42	48	54	60
7	0	7	14	21	28	35	42	49	56	63	70
8	0	8	16	24	32	40	48	56	64	72	80
9	0	9	18	27	36	45	54	63	72	81	90
10	0	10	20	30	40	50	60	70	80	90	100

LOCATE each factor in the multiplication table. The square where the row and column meet shows you the product. WRITE each product.

1.
```
    2
  × 5
   10
```

2.
```
    8
  × 4
   32
```

3.
```
   10
 × 10
  100
```

4.
```
    3
  × 9
   27
```

5.
```
    5
  × 7
   35
```

6.
```
    6
  × 1
    6
```

7.
```
   10
  × 3
   30
```

8.
```
    0
  × 7
    0
```

9.
```
    4
  × 3
   12
```

10.
```
    7
  × 7
   49
```

11.
```
    9
  × 6
   54
```

12.
```
    5
  × 5
   25
```

13.
```
    8
  × 2
   16
```

14.
```
    4
  × 9
   36
```

15.
```
    3
  × 7
   21
```

16.
```
    9
  × 0
    0
```

17.
```
    8
  × 8
   64
```

18.
```
    2
  × 1
    2
```

Computation Station

WRITE each product.

1. 4 × 1 = __4__

2. 7 × 5 = __35__

3. 8 × 3 = __24__

4. 6 × 2 = __12__

5. 9 × 5 = __45__

6. 10 × 2 = __20__

7. 6 × 6 = __36__

8. 1 × 0 = __0__

9. 1 × 8 = __8__

10. 9 × 9 = __81__

11. 7 × 4 = __28__

12. 5 × 3 = __15__

13.
```
  10
×  8
────
  80
```

14.
```
   0
×  2
────
   0
```

15.
```
   9
×  4
────
  36
```

16.
```
   5
×  6
────
  30
```

17.
```
   8
×  2
────
  16
```

18.
```
   4
×  4
────
  16
```

19.
```
   7
×  3
────
  21
```

20.
```
   9
×  8
────
  72
```

21.
```
   4
×  2
────
   8
```

22.
```
   1
×  1
────
   1
```

23.
```
   6
×  3
────
  18
```

24.
```
   9
×  5
────
  45
```

25.
```
   4
×  5
────
  20
```

26.
```
  10
×  4
────
  40
```

27.
```
   0
×  0
────
   0
```

28.
```
   2
×  9
────
  18
```

29.
```
   5
× 10
────
  50
```

30.
```
   3
×  3
────
   9
```

Fair Share

The twins aren't happy unless they get the same number of everything. How many of each toy will they each get? WRITE the answers.

1. ___12___ cars

2. ___10___ marbles

3. ___8___ yo-yos

Sharing Equally

Fair Share

WRITE the number of gems each pirate will get if they split the treasure equally.

$24 \div 4 =$

6 *(crossed out, appears as "6/1")*

1

$8 \div 4 = 2$

4

2

$8 \div 4 = 2$

2

3

$32 \div 4 =$

8

4

Bugged Out

CIRCLE groups of three bugs. WRITE the number of groups in each set.

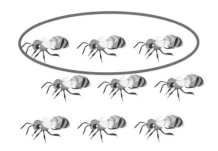

$9 \div 3 =$ __3__
₁

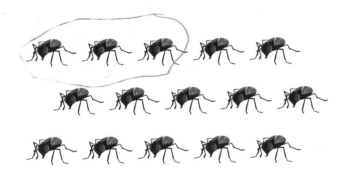

$15 \div 3 =$ __5__
₂

$27 \div 3 =$ __4__
₃

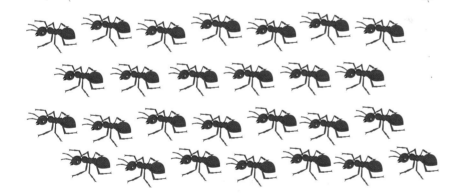

$18 \div 3 =$ __6__
₄

Iced Over

Use the pictures to help you answer each problem. WRITE the answers.

HINT: Count the number of ice cubes in each group.

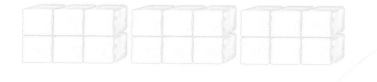

$18 \div 3 = $ _6_

1

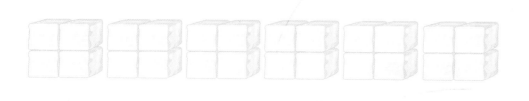

$24 \div 6 = $ ___

2

$25 \div 5 = $ ___

3

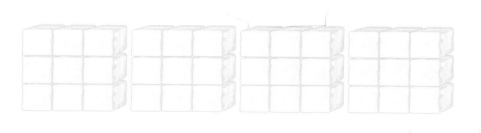

$36 \div 4 = $ ___

4

$20 \div 10 = $ _1_

5

Computation Station

A **quotient** is the number you get when you divide one number by another number. You divide the **dividend** by the **divisor**.

Example:

quotient 6
divisor 3) 18 dividend

×	0	1	2	3	4	5	6	7	8	9	10
0	0	0	0	0	0	0	0	0	0	0	0
1	0	1	2	3	4	5	6	7	8	9	10
2	0	2	4	6	8	10	12	14	16	18	20
3	0	3	6	9	12	15	18	21	24	27	30
4	0	4	8	12	16	20	24	28	32	36	40
5	0	5	10	15	20	25	30	35	40	45	50
6	0	6	12	18	24	30	36	42	48	54	60
7	0	7	14	21	28	35	42	49	56	63	70
8	0	8	16	24	32	40	48	56	64	72	80
9	0	9	18	27	36	45	54	63	72	81	90
10	0	10	20	30	40	50	60	70	80	90	100

WRITE each quotient.

1. 2) 16

2. 8) 24

3. 9) 90

4. 1) 7

5. 3) 21

6. 7) 14

7. 5) 35

8. 7) 56

9. 4) 32

10. 8) 48

11. 9) 81

12. 2) 12

13. 7) 63

14. 1) 3

15. 10) 70

16. 3) 9

17. 9) 36

18. 4) 40

Dividing

Computation Station

WRITE each quotient.

1. $20 \div 5 =$ _____   2. $80 \div 8 =$ _____   3. $12 \div 6 =$ 1

4. $18 \div 2 =$ 5 5. $24 \div 3 =$ _____   6. $30 \div 6 =$ _____

7. $90 \div 10 =$ _____   8. $56 \div 8 =$ _____   9. $36 \div 6 =$ _____

10. $45 \div 5 =$ _____   11. $16 \div 4 =$ 4 12. $3 \div 1 =$ 1

13. $5 \overline{)15}$ 14. $5 \overline{)25}$ 15. $6 \overline{)24}$ 16. $10 \overline{)60}$ 17. $9 \overline{)72}$ 18. $1 \overline{)8}$

19. $2 \overline{)6}$ 20. $4 \overline{)40}$ 21. $7 \overline{)63}$ 22. $4 \overline{)28}$ 23. $3 \overline{)27}$ 24. $7 \overline{)49}$

25. $6 \overline{)54}$ 26. $7 \overline{)14}$ 27. $3 \overline{)30}$ 28. $9 \overline{)45}$ 29. $6 \overline{)48}$ 30. $5 \overline{)20}$

Factor Hunt

WRITE all of the factors of each number. Use the multiplication table to help you.

HINT: Write down all of the numbers that can be used to divide each number evenly. Remember that every number can be divided by itself and 1.

Example:

10 | 1 | 2 | 5 | 10 |

×	0	1	2	3	4	5	6	7	8	9	10
0	0	0	0	0	0	0	0	0	0	0	0
1	0	1	2	3	4	5	6	7	8	9	10
2	0	2	4	6	8	10	12	14	16	18	20
3	0	3	6	9	12	15	18	21	24	27	30
4	0	4	8	12	16	20	24	28	32	36	40
5	0	5	10	15	20	25	30	35	40	45	50
6	0	6	12	18	24	30	36	42	48	54	60
7	0	7	14	21	28	35	42	49	56	63	70
8	0	8	16	24	32	40	48	56	64	72	80
9	0	9	18	27	36	45	54	63	72	81	90
10	0	10	20	30	40	50	60	70	80	90	100

1. 4

2. 6

3. 9

4. 12

5. 15

6. 16

7. 18

Tic-Tac-Toe

A **multiple** is a number that can be divided evenly by another number. CIRCLE any number that is a multiple of the blue number. PUT an X through any number that is not a multiple. DRAW a line when you find three multiples in a row. The line can go across, down, or diagonally.

Example:

5

42	10	24
16	35	40
25	5	81

5

42	⑩	24
16	㉟	㊵
㉕	⑤	81

Multiples of 5 are
5, 10, 15, 20, 25,
30, 35, 40, 45, 50.

2

12	18	16
4	7	9
3	15	20

10

55	20	49
70	36	72
50	80	30

6

40	14	12
25	54	36
63	8	18

8

56	36	24
27	80	64
48	34	30

Work It Out

Each Roaring Racetrack set comes with 10 straight tracks, 8 curved tracks, 3 track loops, and 4 cars.

1. How many pieces are in 5 Roaring Racetrack sets?

   Straight tracks _____

   Curved tracks _____

   Track loops _____

   Cars _____

Jonah invited 6 friends over for hot dogs. Each of his friends can eat 3 hot dogs.

2. How many hot dogs does Jonah need to make? _____

Work It Out

Felix bought a box of 36 dog biscuits and 12 cans of dog food for his 6 dogs.

1. If each dog gets the same amount, how much food will each dog get?

   _____ dog biscuits

   _____ cans of food

Zoë has 64 stickers and a sticker album with 8 pages.

2. If she puts the same number of stickers on each page, how many stickers

   will be on 1 page? _____

Computation Station

WRITE each product.

1.
  3
× 5

2.
  9
× 8

3.
  6
× 4

4.
  5
× 1

5.
  7
× 0

6.
  10
× 2

7.
  8
× 8

8.
  3
× 3

9.
  5
× 9

10.
  2
× 8

11.
  7
× 9

12.
  4
× 7

13.
  9
× 4

14.
  10
× 6

15.
  0
× 9

16.
  6
× 8

17.
  9
× 9

18.
  6
× 3

WRITE each quotient.

19. 5)20

20. 7)42

21. 3)15

22. 10)70

23. 9)9

24. 6)12

25. 2)18

26. 8)56

27. 9)90

28. 7)21

29. 6)36

30. 4)12

31. 5)25

32. 4)8

33. 7)28

34. 4)32

35. 9)27

36. 5)35

Fact Finder

WRITE all of the multiplication and division number sentences that go with each picture.

Example:

3 rows of 4 jellybeans = 12 total jellybeans

3	×	4	=	12
4	×	3	=	12
12	÷	3	=	4
12	÷	4	=	3

1.

_____ × _____ = _____

_____ × _____ = _____

_____ ÷ _____ = _____

_____ ÷ _____ = _____

2.

_____ × _____ = _____

_____ × _____ = _____

_____ ÷ _____ = _____

_____ ÷ _____ = _____

3.

_____ × _____ = _____

_____ × _____ = _____

_____ ÷ _____ = _____

_____ ÷ _____ = _____

4.

_____ × _____ = _____

_____ × _____ = _____

_____ ÷ _____ = _____

_____ ÷ _____ = _____

Any Way You Slice It

WRITE the fraction for each picture.

Example:

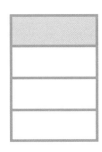

$\dfrac{1}{4}$ ← the number of shaded sections
← the total number of sections

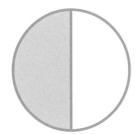

_____
1

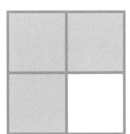

_____
2

_____
3

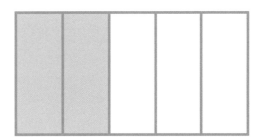

_____
4

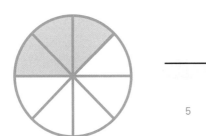

_____
5

_____
6

Piece of Cake

COLOR the cake pieces to match each fraction.

$\dfrac{1}{3}$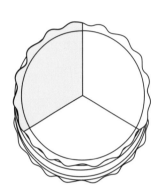

$\dfrac{3}{4}$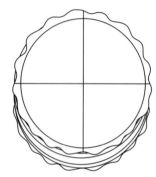

$\dfrac{4}{5}$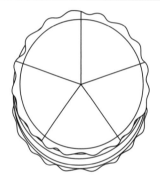

$\dfrac{5}{8}$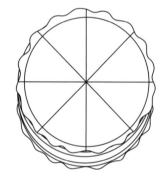

$\dfrac{2}{7}$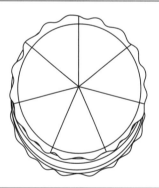

$\dfrac{3}{10}$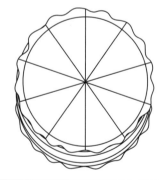

$\dfrac{1}{6}$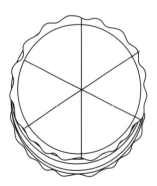

$\dfrac{7}{8}$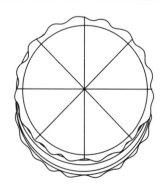

Fraction Bars

WRITE the fraction for each picture.

1. _____

2. _____

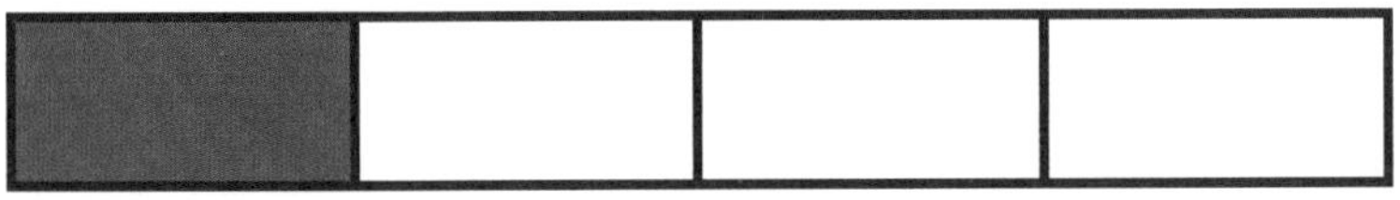

3. _____

4. _____

5. _____

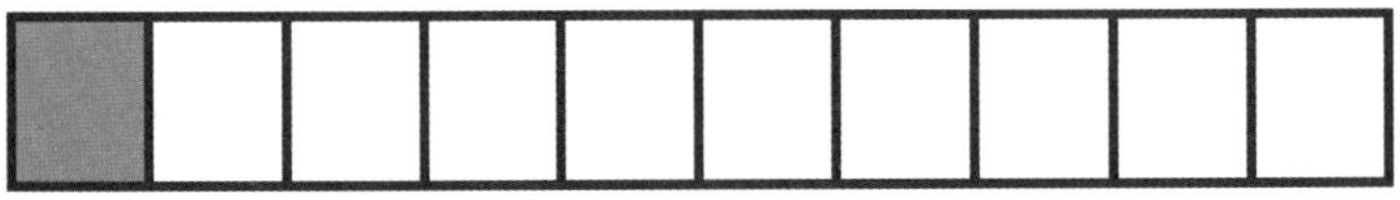

6. _____

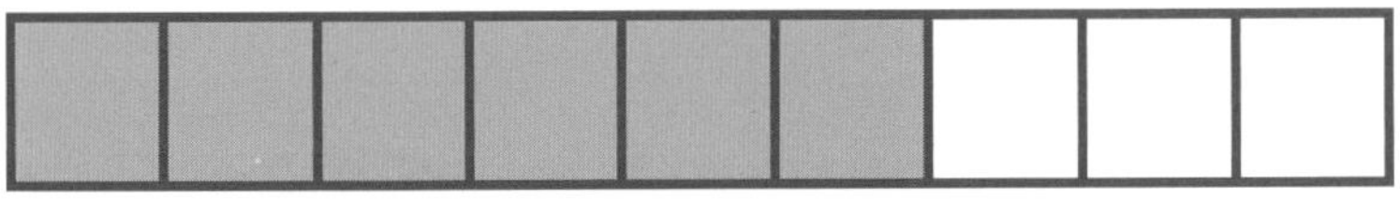

7. _____

8. _____

Parts of a Whole

Odd One Out

CROSS OUT the picture or fraction in each row that does **not** match the others.

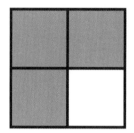 $\dfrac{3}{4}$    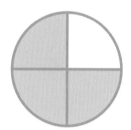

$\dfrac{5}{6}$ 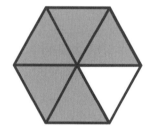      

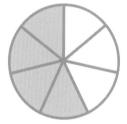   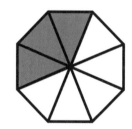   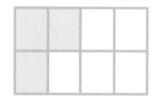 $\dfrac{3}{8}$

   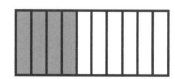 $\dfrac{4}{9}$ 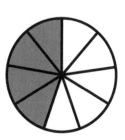

Shaded Shapes

WRITE the fraction for each set.

Example: $\dfrac{5}{6}$ ← the number of shaded circles
← the total number of circles

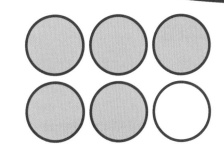

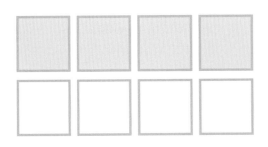
_____ 1

_____ 2

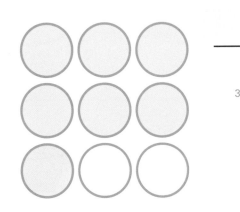
_____ 3

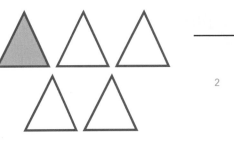
_____ 4

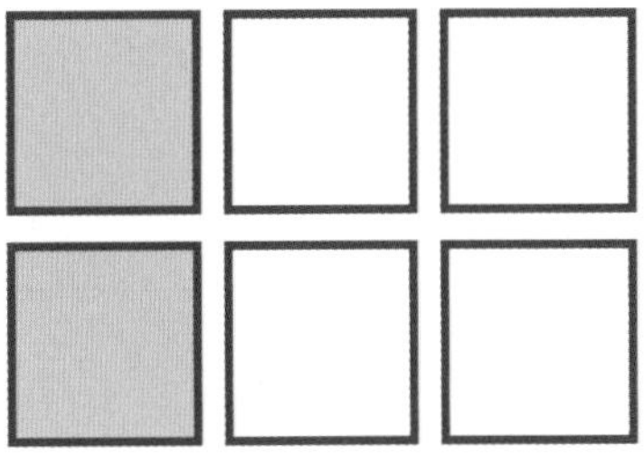

_____ 5

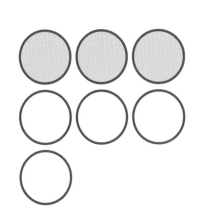
_____ 6

Parts of a Set

Jellybean Jars

COLOR each jar of jellybeans.

$\frac{3}{7}$ green

$\frac{4}{7}$ blue

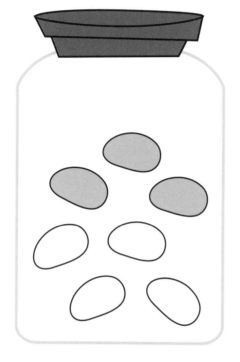

$\frac{1}{8}$ purple

$\frac{2}{8}$ green

$\frac{5}{8}$ orange

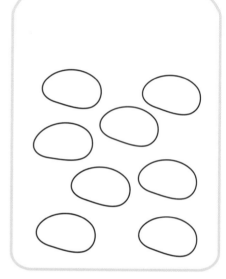

$\frac{2}{10}$ red

$\frac{3}{10}$ yellow

$\frac{5}{10}$ purple

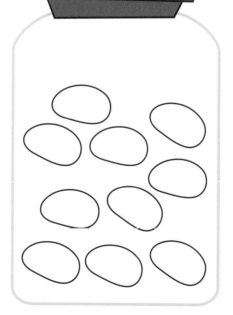

$\frac{1}{9}$ orange

$\frac{2}{9}$ red

$\frac{3}{9}$ blue

$\frac{3}{9}$ purple

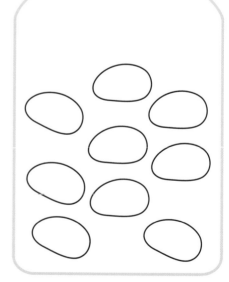

Fashion Fractions

WRITE the fraction for each description.

1. Fraction of kids wearing orange shirts

$$\frac{3}{7}$$

2. Fraction of kids wearing hats —————

3. Fraction of girls wearing skirts —————

4. Fraction of boys wearing sunglasses —————

5. Fraction of girls with red hair —————

6. Fraction of boys wearing shorts —————

Find the Same

CIRCLE the picture in each row that matches the fraction.

$\frac{4}{5}$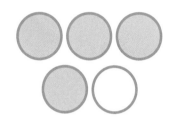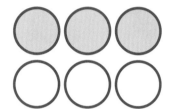

$\frac{7}{9}$

$\frac{1}{6}$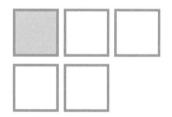

$\frac{3}{10}$

Piece of Cake

COLOR the cake pieces to match each fraction. Then CIRCLE the larger fraction.

HINT: The larger fraction is the one with more cake colored.

$\dfrac{1}{6}$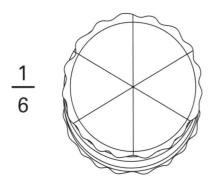

$\dfrac{1}{5}$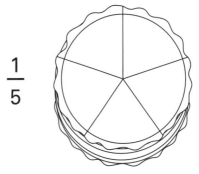

$\dfrac{4}{7}$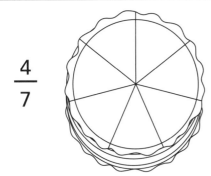

$\dfrac{3}{8}$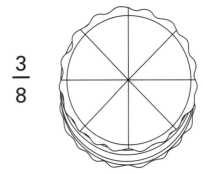

$\dfrac{1}{4}$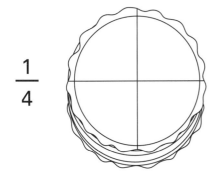

$\dfrac{2}{9}$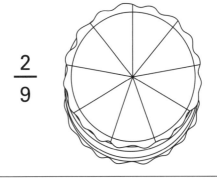

$\dfrac{7}{10}$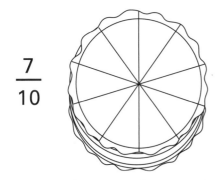

$\dfrac{7}{8}$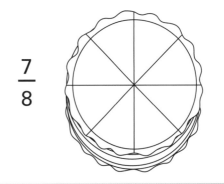

Comparing Fractions

Matched or Mismatched?

WRITE >, <, or = in each box.

HINT: Use the fraction bars to help you picture the fractions.

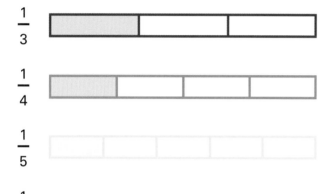

$\frac{1}{3}$

$\frac{1}{4}$

$\frac{1}{5}$

$\frac{1}{6}$

$\frac{1}{7}$

$\frac{1}{8}$

$\frac{1}{9}$

$\frac{1}{10}$

$\frac{2}{5}$ ☐ $\frac{1}{4}$
    1

$\frac{5}{6}$ ☐ $\frac{1}{3}$
    2

$\frac{1}{6}$ ☐ $\frac{4}{9}$
    3

$\frac{4}{8}$ ☐ $\frac{5}{10}$
    4

$\frac{7}{10}$ ☐ $\frac{7}{8}$
    5

$\frac{4}{4}$ ☐ $\frac{5}{8}$
    6

$\frac{5}{9}$ ☐ $\frac{6}{9}$
    7

$\frac{2}{7}$ ☐ $\frac{2}{4}$
    8

$\frac{5}{9}$ ☐ $\frac{4}{10}$
    9

$\frac{3}{6}$ ☐ $\frac{3}{7}$
    10

$\frac{5}{7}$ ☐ $\frac{5}{8}$
    11

$\frac{7}{7}$ ☐ $\frac{9}{9}$
    12

Match Up

WRITE the number next to each fraction. Then DRAW lines to match fractions that are the same.

_____   _____

_____   _____

_____   _____

_____   _____

_____   _____

_____   _____

Matched or Mismatched?

COLOR the pictures to match each fraction. Then WRITE >, <, or = in each box.

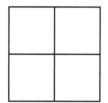 $\dfrac{3}{4}$ ☐ $\dfrac{2}{4}$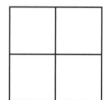

 $\dfrac{3}{7}$ ☐ $\dfrac{5}{7}$

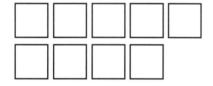 $\dfrac{2}{4}$ ☐ $\dfrac{3}{6}$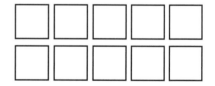

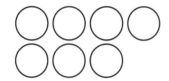 $\dfrac{3}{9}$ ☐ $\dfrac{7}{10}$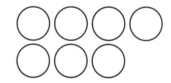

 $\dfrac{5}{8}$ ☐ $\dfrac{5}{9}$

Measure Up

WRITE the approximate length of each object in inches (in.) and centimeters (cm).

1. about _____ in.   about _____ cm

2. about _____ in.   about _____ cm

3. about _____ in.   about _____ cm

4. about _____ in.   about _____ cm

Length

Rulers Rule

MEASURE each piece of ribbon with a ruler. WRITE the approximate length of each object in inches (in.) and centimeters (cm).

1.

about _____ in.   about _____ cm

2.

about _____ in.   about _____ cm

3.

about _____ in.   about _____ cm

4.

about _____ in.   about _____ cm

5.

about _____ in.   about _____ cm

6.

about _____ in.   about _____ cm

Preferred Measure

Which unit of measure would you use to measure each object? CIRCLE *inch*, *foot*, or *yard*.

NOTE: These rulers show how the units compare to each other. They are not actual size.

inch

foot

yard

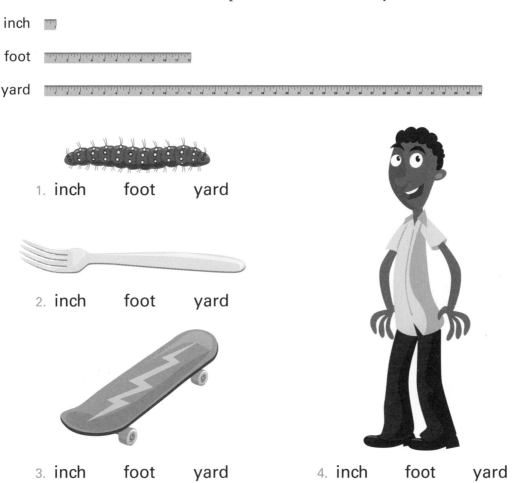

1. inch   foot   yard

2. inch   foot   yard

3. inch   foot   yard

4. inch   foot   yard

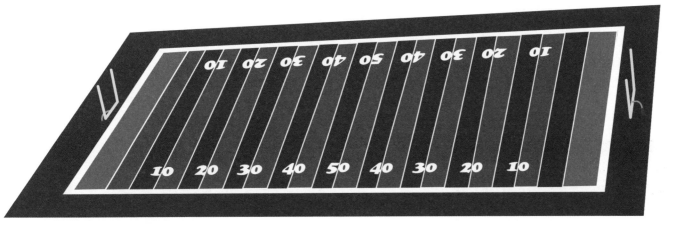

5. inch   foot   yard

Length

Which Is Best?

Which is the best unit to measure the length of each object? CIRCLE *centimeter* or *meter*.

NOTE: These rulers show how the units compare to each other. They are not actual size.

centimeter

meter

1. centimeter   meter

2. centimeter   meter

3. centimeter   meter

4. centimeter   meter

5. centimeter   meter

6. centimeter   meter

Match Up

DRAW lines to match the pictures with equal amounts of liquid volume.

Example:

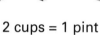 

2 cups = 1 pint   2 pints = 1 quart   4 quarts = 1 gallon

Liquid Volume

Which Is Best?

Which is the best unit to measure the liquid volume of each object? CIRCLE *cup*, *pint*, *quart*, or *gallon*.

1. cup   pint   quart   gallon

2. cup   pint   quart   gallon

3. cup   pint   quart   gallon

4. cup   pint   quart   gallon

5. cup   pint   quart   gallon

6. cup   pint   quart   gallon

7. cup   pint   quart   gallon

8. cup   pint   quart   gallon

Circle the Same

CIRCLE any item that can hold at least 1 liter of liquid.

Example:

1 liter (1 L)
1 liter = 1,000 milliliters

120 milliliters (120 mL)

Which Is Best?

Which is the best unit to measure the liquid volume of each object? CIRCLE *milliliter* or *liter*.

1.   milliliter   liter

2.   milliliter   liter

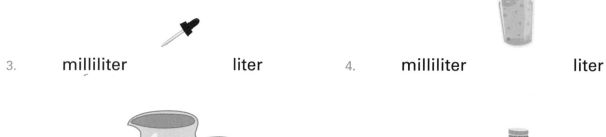

3.   milliliter   liter

4.   milliliter   liter

5.   milliliter   liter

6.   milliliter   liter

7.   milliliter   liter

8.   milliliter   liter

Circle It

CIRCLE any item that weighs less than 1 pound.

Example:

1 pound (1 lb)
1 pound = 16 ounces

1 ounce (1 oz)

Which Is Best?

Which is the best unit to measure the weight of each object? CIRCLE *ounce* or *pound*.

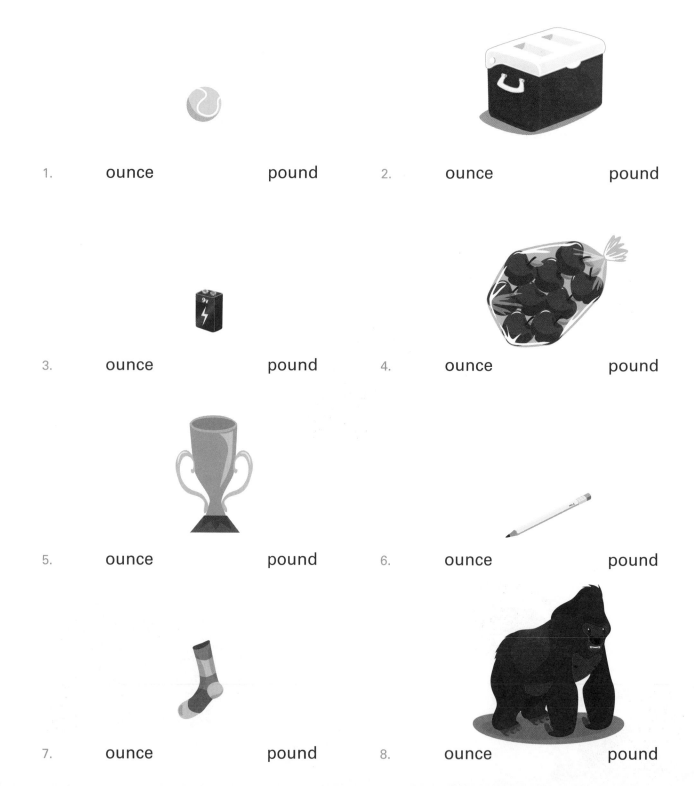

1.   ounce   pound   2.   ounce   pound

3.   ounce   pound   4.   ounce   pound

5.   ounce   pound   6.   ounce   pound

7.   ounce   pound   8.   ounce   pound

Circle It

CIRCLE any item that weighs more than 1 kilogram.

Example:

1 kilogram (1 kg)
1 kilogram = 1,000 grams

1 gram (1 g)

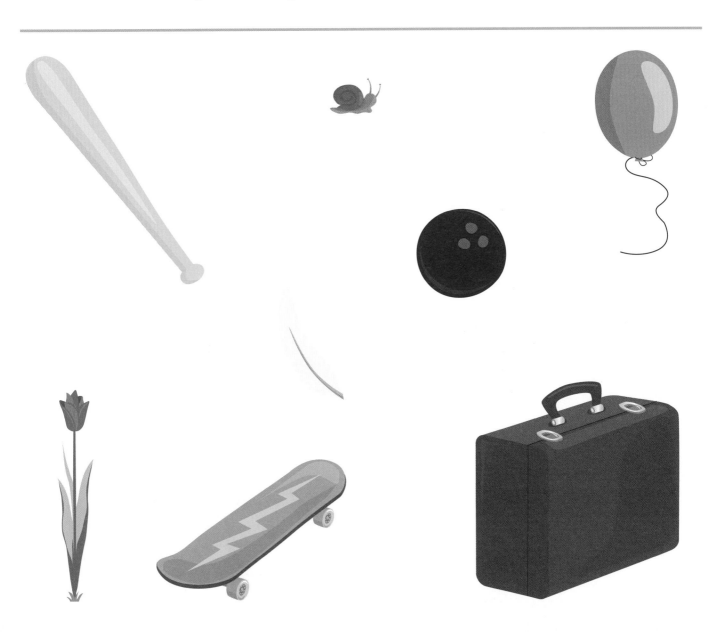

Which Is Best?

Which is the best unit to measure the weight of each object? CIRCLE *gram* or *kilogram*.

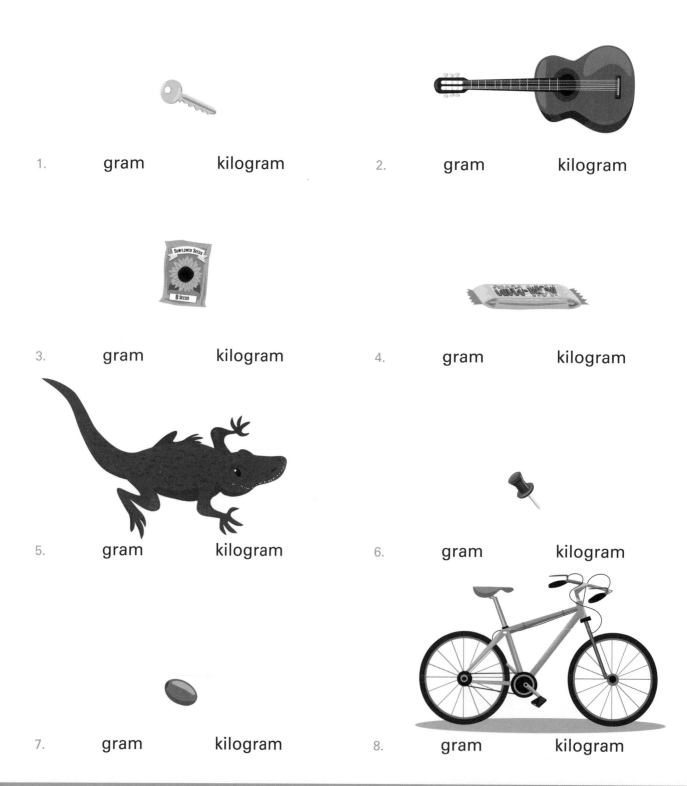

1. gram   kilogram

2. gram   kilogram

3. gram   kilogram

4. gram   kilogram

5. gram   kilogram

6. gram   kilogram

7. gram   kilogram

8. gram   kilogram

Measure Up

MEASURE each temperature to the nearest degree. WRITE the temperature in degrees
Fahrenheit (°F) and degrees Celsius (°C).

Example:

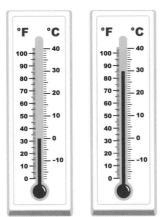

Water freezes at 32°F or 0°C.
A hot summer day might be 86°F or 30°C.

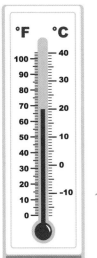

1. _____ °F

_____ °C

2. _____ °F

_____ °C

3. _____ °F

_____ °C

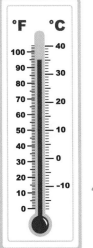

4. _____ °F

_____ °C

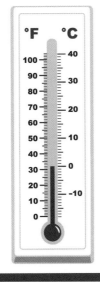

5. _____ °F

_____ °C

6. _____ °F

_____ °C

Circle It

CIRCLE the appropriate item of clothing for the weather shown on each thermometer.

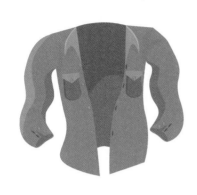

Rulers Rule

WRITE the approximate length of each worm in inches (in.) and centimeters (cm).

1. about _____ in.   about _____ cm

2. about _____ in.   about _____ cm

3. about _____ in.   about _____ cm

4. about _____ in.   about _____ cm

Measuring Mash-up

CIRCLE the best unit of measure for each object.

1.   ounce   pound

2.   gallon   pint

3.   gram   kilogram

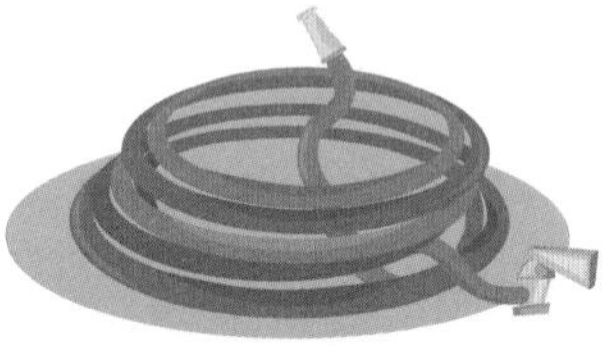

4.   yard   inch

5.   quart   cup

6.   pint   gallon

7.   liter   milliliter

8.   centimeter   meter

Matched or Mismatched?

WRITE >, <, or = in each box.

1 centimeter	▢ 1	1 meter
1 gallon	▢ 2	1 pint
1 kilogram	▢ 3	1,000 grams
1 yard	▢ 4	1 foot
2 pints	▢ 5	1 quart
15 ounces	▢ 6	1 pound
1 yard	▢ 7	6 inches
50 milliliters	▢ 8	1 liter
3,000 grams	▢ 9	1 kilogram
1 foot	▢ 10	12 inches
5 cups	▢ 11	3 pints
6 quarts	▢ 12	1 gallon

Measuring Mash-up

CIRCLE the best unit of measure for each object.

1. **Length of a speedboat**   centimeter   meter   inch

2. **Body temperature**   gram   milliliter   degrees

3. **Weight of a caterpillar**   pound   yard   gram

4. **Volume of a drinking glass**   cup   gallon   kilogram

5. **Weight of a baby**   gram   pound   quart

6. **Length of a toe**   centimeter   foot   meter

7. **Volume of a washing machine**   milliliter   gallon   cup

8. **Length of a shoelace**   yard   meter   inch

Matched Set

COLOR all of the shapes in each row that match the word.

HINT: A square is a special type of rectangle.

circle

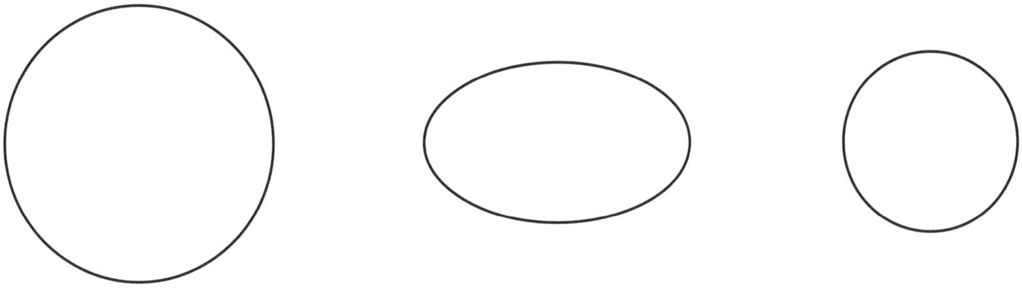

square

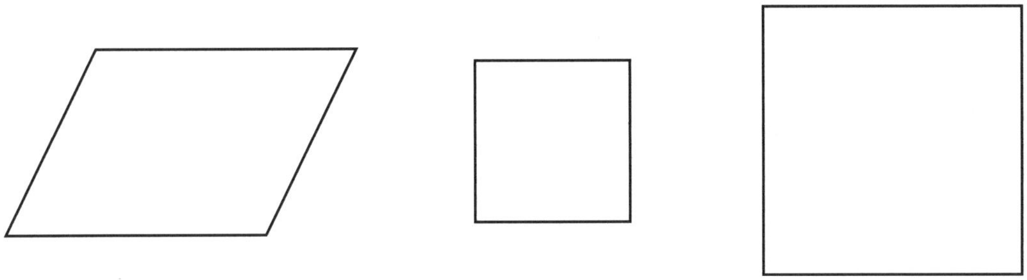

triangle

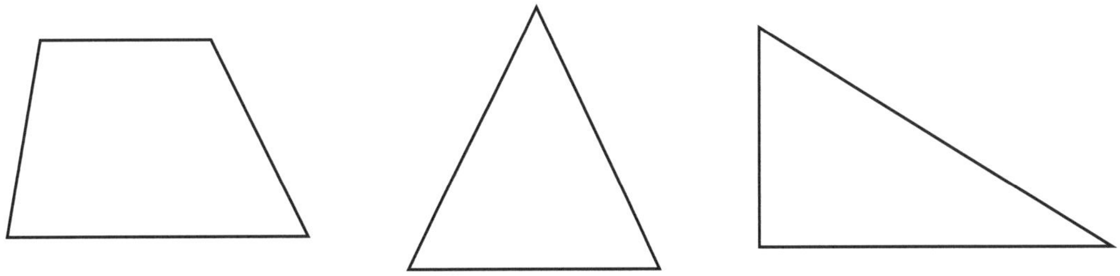

rectangle

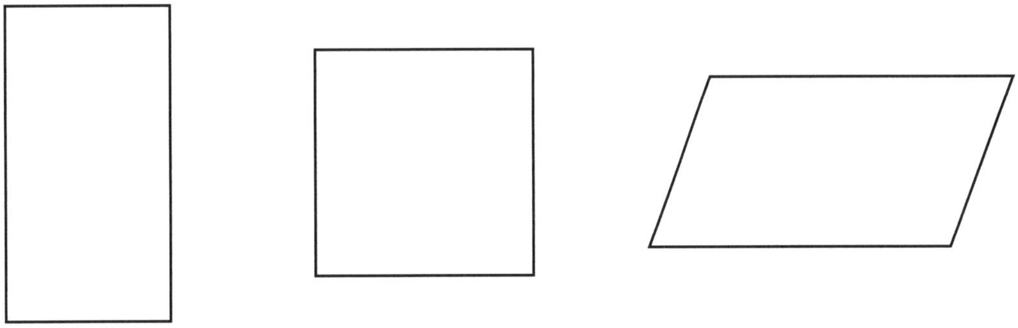

Plane Shapes

Shape Up

A **vertex** is where two lines meet. A **side** is the line between two vertices.

Example:

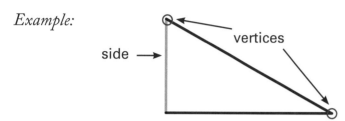

side ➝

vertices

WRITE the number of vertices and sides for each shape.

	Number of Vertices	Number of Sides

Around We Go

Perimeter is the distance around a two-dimensional shape. To find the perimeter, add all of the side lengths. For shapes with sides that are all the same length, multiply the length of one side by the number of sides.

Example:

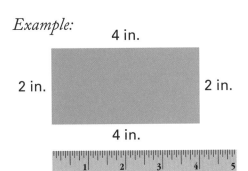

4 + 2 + 4 + 2 = 12
The perimeter of this rectangle is 12 in.

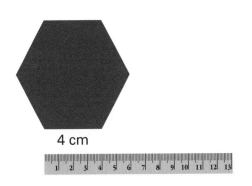

4 x 6 = 24
The perimeter of this hexagon is 24 cm.

WRITE the perimeter of each shape.

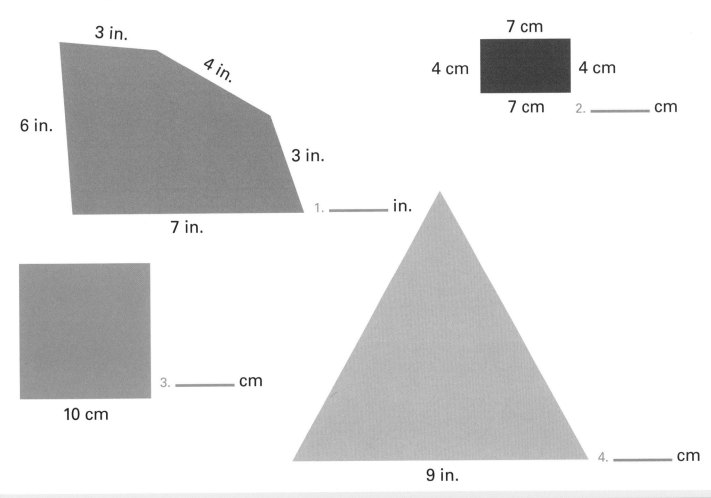

1. _____ in.

2. _____ cm

3. _____ cm

4. _____ cm

Squared Away

Area is the size of the surface of a shape, and it is measured in square units. WRITE the area of each shape.

Example:

1 square unit

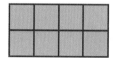

To find the area, multiply the height by the width. This rectangle is 2 square units high by 4 square units wide. 2 x 4 = 8.

The area of this rectangle is 8 square units.

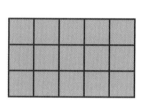

1. _____ square units

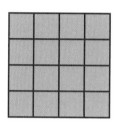

2. _____ square units

3. _____ square units

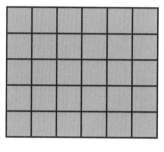

4. _____ square units

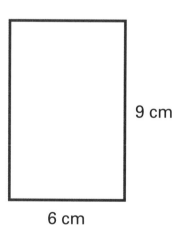

9 cm

6 cm

5. _____ sq cm

5 in.

6. _____ sq in.

Find the Same

CIRCLE the object in each row that is the same shape as the first shape.

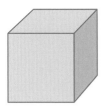   

Odd One Out

CROSS OUT the shape in each row that is **not** the same as the others.

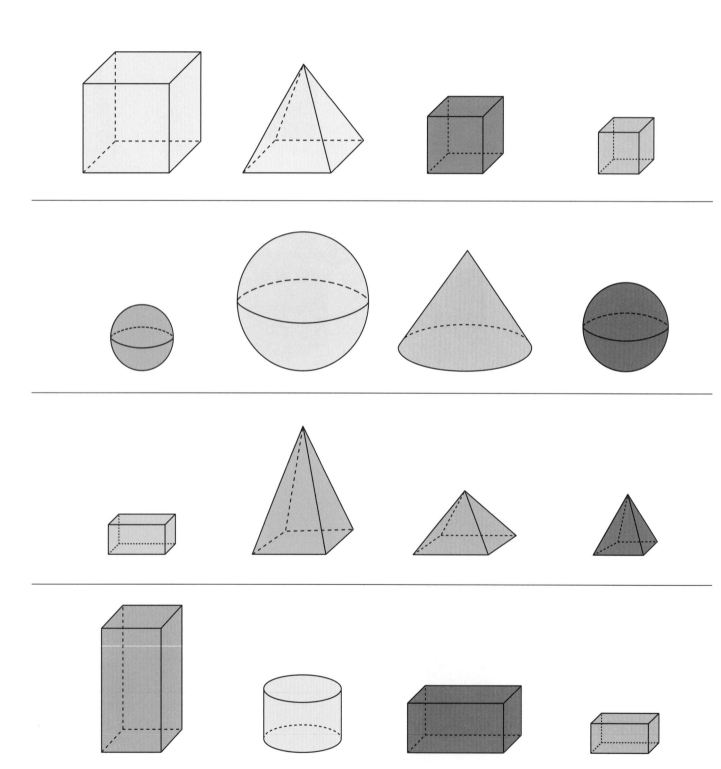

Shape Up

In a three-dimensional shape, a **vertex** is where three or more edges meet. An **edge** is where two sides meet. A **face** is the shape formed by the edges.

WRITE the number of vertices, edges, and faces for each shape.

	Number of Vertices	Number of Edges	Number of Faces

About Face

CIRCLE all of the shapes that are faces on the three-dimensional shape.

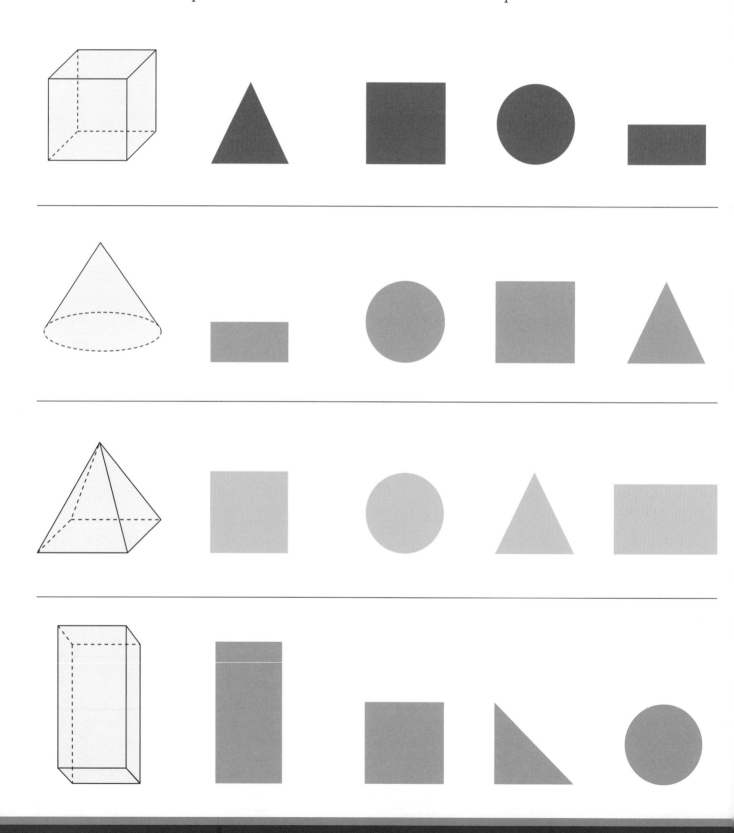

Mirror, Mirror

DRAW a line of symmetry through each picture.

HINT: Some shapes have more than one line of symmetry.

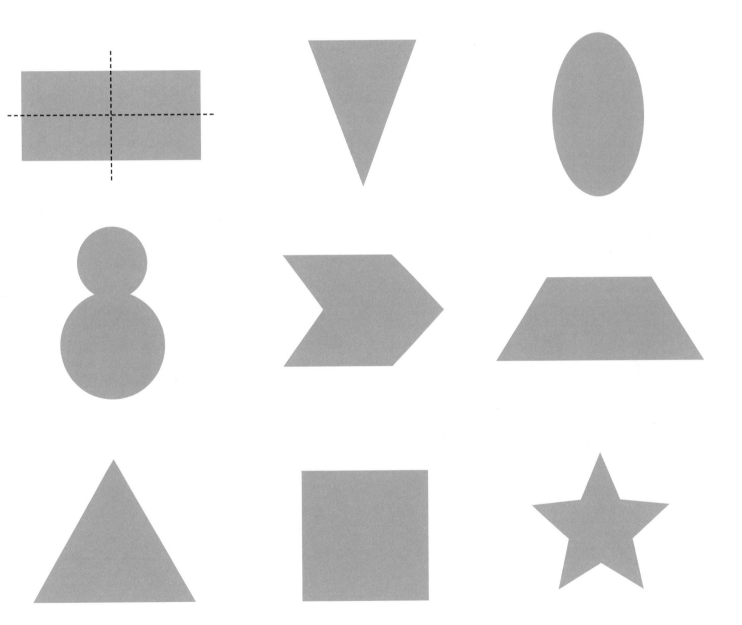

Color Flip

COLOR the pictures so they are symmetrical.

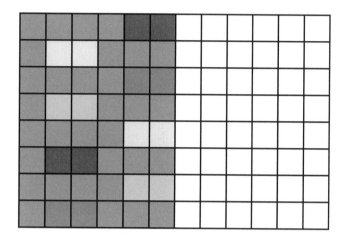

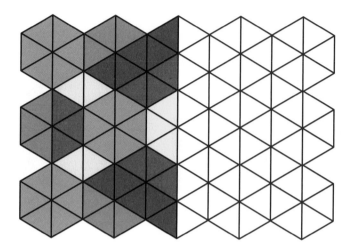

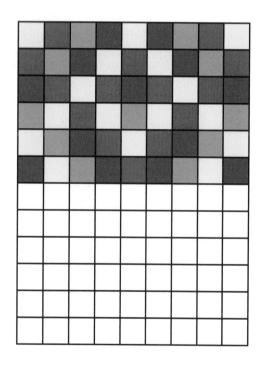

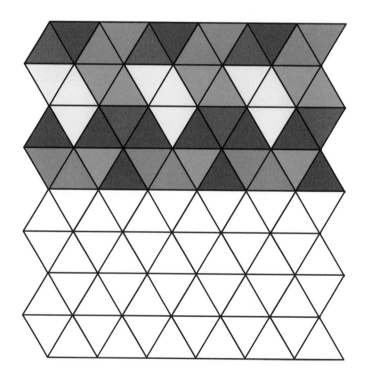

Any Which Way

A **flip**, **slide**, or **turn** has been applied to each shape. WRITE *flip*, *slide*, or *turn* for each pair of shapes.

Example:

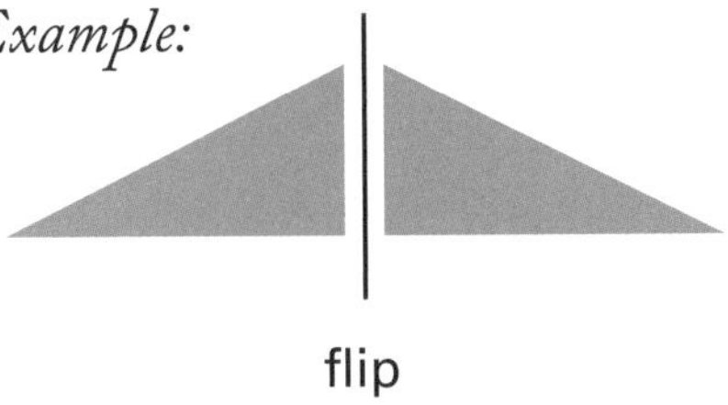

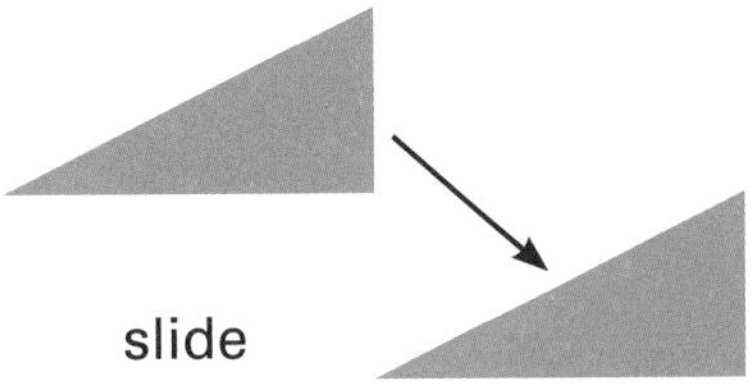

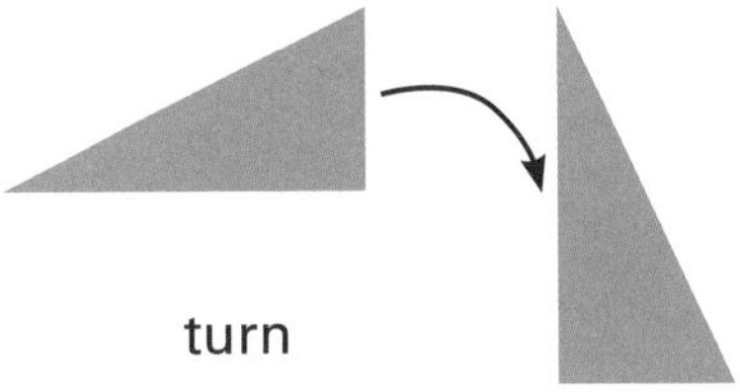

flip   slide   turn

1

2

3

4

5

6

7

8

Perfect Patterns

A **tessellation** is a repeating pattern of shapes that has no gaps or overlapping shapes. DRAW and COLOR the rest of each tessellation.

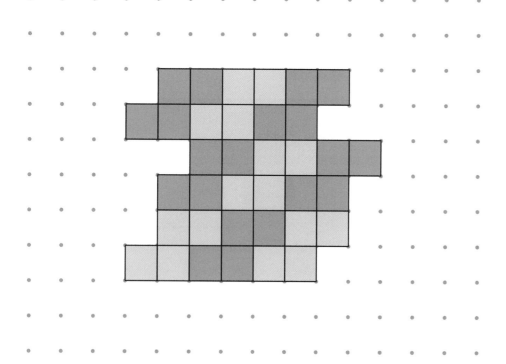

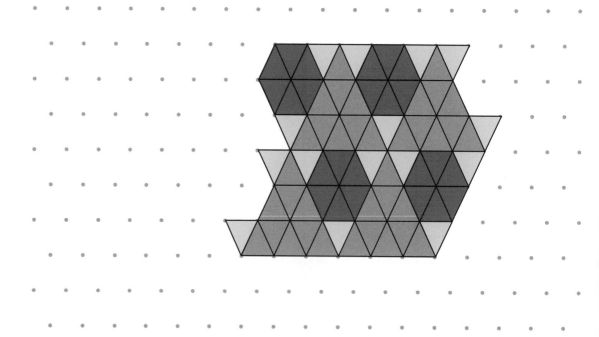

Match Up

DRAW a line to match each shape to its description.

8 sides
8 vertices

5 sides
5 vertices

6 sides
6 vertices

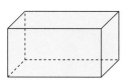

8 edges
5 vertices
5 faces

6 edges
4 vertices
4 faces

12 edges
8 vertices
6 faces

Unit Rewind

WRITE the perimeter and area of this rectangle.

1.

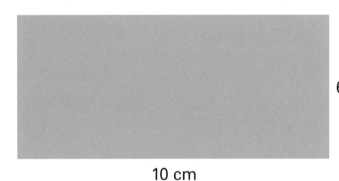

6 cm

10 cm

Perimeter: _____ cm

Area: _____ sq cm

DRAW the line or lines of symmetry through each letter.

2. A

3. D

4. X

WRITE *flip*, *slide*, or *turn*.

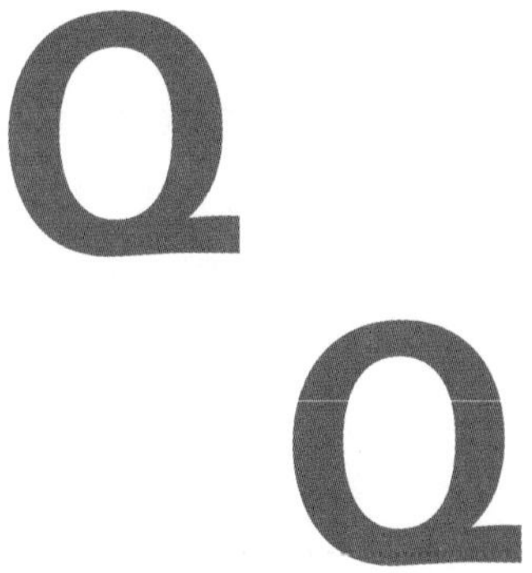

Q Q

Z N

R R

_____
5

_____
6

_____
7

It's about Time

WRITE the time on each clock.

Example:

_____5_____ : _____37_____

1. _____ : _____

2. _____ : _____

3. _____ : _____

4. _____ : _____

5. _____ : _____

6. _____ : _____

Telling Time

Watch It!

DRAW a line to connect each watch to a clock that shows the same time.

Set Your Clock

Each clock has the wrong time. DRAW hands to show the correct time on each clock.

HINT: Add time to a clock that is slow, and subtract time from a clock that is fast.

1.

   1 hour and 41 minutes slow   ⟶

2.

   2 hours and 27 minutes slow   ⟶

3.

   1 hour and 16 minutes fast   ⟶

4.

   3 hours and 45 minutes fast   ⟶

Adding & Subtracting Time

Time Difference

WRITE the difference in time between each pair of clocks.

1.

1:17

5:58

_____ hours _____ minutes

2.

10:43

12:47

_____ hours _____ minutes

3.

6:36

9:09

_____ hours _____ minutes

4.

7:24

11:11

_____ hours _____ minutes

Tick Tock, Tick Tock

Jake follows the same schedule every day. How much time does he spend doing each activity in five days?

HINT: Multiply each time by 5.

ONE DAY

Eating	1 hour
Watching TV	1 hour 30 minutes
Going to school	6 hours 45 minutes
Reading	45 minutes
Playing soccer	2 hours 15 minutes
Sleeping	8 hours 20 minutes

FIVE DAYS

1. Eating   _____ hours _____ minutes

2. Watching TV   _____ hours _____ minutes

3. Going to school   _____ hours _____ minutes

4. Reading   _____ hours _____ minutes

5. Playing soccer   _____ hours _____ minutes

6. Sleeping   _____ hours _____ minutes

Mad Dash

WRITE how long it took for each person to run one mile. CIRCLE the person who had the fastest time per mile.

HINT: Divide the total time by the number of miles.

 5 miles: 45 minutes

1. 1 mile: _____ minutes

 2 miles: 20 minutes

2. 1 mile: _____ minutes

 8 miles: 64 minutes

3. 1 mile: _____ minutes

 3 miles: 18 minutes

4. 1 mile: _____ minutes

 10 miles: 1 hour 10 minutes

5. 1 mile: _____ minutes

 7 miles: 56 minutes

6. 1 mile: _____ minutes

Cash Crunch

WRITE the total cost to buy all four items.

HINT: Use the money to help you add.

$48

$63.50

$75

$12.25

Total cost _____

Adding & Subtracting Money

Making Change

Using the money to buy each item, how much change will you get back? WRITE the answer for each item.

1.  $1.18

Change: _____

2.  $4.45

Change: _____

3. $28.30

Change: _____

4. $82.64

Change: _____

Filling Orders

WRITE the total cost of each order.

GUEST CHECK

Date	Table	Guests	Server	000903
4	Galaxy Burgers			
2	Sunburst Salads			
1	Freaky Fries			
3	Milky Way Milkshakes			
			Total	

GUEST CHECK

Date	Table	Guests	Server	000904
3	Pluto Burgers			
5	Black Hole Burgers			
2	Milky Way Milkshakes			
4	Mars Waters			
			Total	

GUEST CHECK

Date	Table	Guests	Server	000905
4	Galaxy Burgers			
9	Pluto Burgers			
3	Sunburst Salads			
6	Freaky Fries			
5	Mars Waters			
			Total	

GUEST CHECK

Date	Table	Guests	Server	000906
2	Pluto Burgers			
8	Black Hole Burgers			
2	Sunburst Salads			
5	Freaky Fries			
4	Milky Way Milkshakes			
			Total	

Best Price

WRITE the cost of one marble. CIRCLE the bag that has the lowest price for one marble.

1.

$36.00

1 marble: _____

2.

$4.50

1 marble: _____

3.

$9.00

1 marble: _____

4.
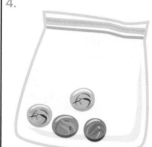
$20.00

1 marble: _____

5.

$20.00

1 marble: _____

6.

$14.00

1 marble: _____

7.
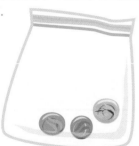
$12.75

1 marble: _____

8.

$24.00

1 marble: _____

Work It Out

WRITE the answers.

Rita spent 42 minutes riding her bike into town, 28 minutes at the comic book store, 11 minutes at the ice cream shop with her friends, and 54 minutes on the bike ride home.

1. How long was Rita gone? _____ hours _____ minutes

2. If Rita left the house at 3:00, what time did she return home? _____:_____

John goes to the hardware store and buys a hammer for $17.00, 3 screwdrivers for $9.00 each, and 10 screws for 10 cents a piece.

3. How much money does John spend? _____

Joelle makes her own necklaces. Each necklace takes 15 minutes to make and costs her $8.00 in supplies.

4. How long does it take to make 12 necklaces? _____

5. How much would Joelle spend to make 7 necklaces? _____

Unit Rewind

WRITE the time on each clock. Then WRITE the difference in time between them.

1. _____ : _____   _____ : _____   _____ hours _____ minutes

2. _____ : _____   _____ : _____   _____ hours _____ minutes

3. CIRCLE the box with the best price for one donut.

 $12.00    $15.00    $24.00

4. How much would eight robots cost?

$8.00

_____

5. How much would five packs of gum cost?

50¢

_____

Answers

Page 3
1. 5, 0, 8, 1   2. 6, 3, 3, 7
3. 0, 4, 2, 8   4. 9, 9, 6, 3
5. 2, 0, 0, 6   6. 3, 7, 1, 2

Page 4
1. six thousand, four hundred five
2. one thousand, five hundred thirty-eight
3. two thousand, seven hundred eighty
4. four thousand, nine hundred ninety-nine
5. seven thousand, two hundred sixty-three
6. nine thousand, three hundred fourteen
7. 3,576   8. 8,633
9. 5,210   10. 9,891
11. 7,345   12. 1,452

Page 5
1. 3,345   2. 8,229   3. 5,674
4. 1,963   5. 4,516   6. 6,437

Page 6
1. 7,481   2. 2,356   3. 6,292
4. 4,623   5. 9,108   6. 5,534

Page 7
1. <   2. >   3. >
4. <   5. <   6. >
7. >   8. <   9. <
10. >   11. <   12. >
13. >   14. <   15. <

Pages 8
1. >   2. <   3. =
4. >   5. =   6. <

Pages 9
1. 6,672   2. 9,158   3. 5,803
4. 4,910   5. 7,398   6. 3,848

Page 10
1. 4,763   2. 7,848   3. 3,399
4. 6,332   5. 2,165   6. 9,528

Page 11
1. 20   2. 90   3. 40
4. 90   5. 50   6. 80
7. 20   8. 40   9. 500
10. 400 11. 100 12. 800
13. 500 14. 800 15. 600
16. 300

Page 12
1. 7,000   2. 1,000   3. 6,000
4. 8,000   5. 3,000   6. 6,000
7. 9,000   8. 3,000   9. 2,000
10. 4,000 11. 8,000 12. 6,000
13. 4,000 14. 3,000 15. 7,000
16. 4,000

Page 13
Check:
1. $16   2. $240   3. $3,200

Page 14
Check: 167

Page 15
1. 8,421   2. 3,954
3. 5,736   4. 7,677
5. four thousand, three hundred eighty-five

Page 15 (continued)
6. six thousand, five hundred nine
7. seven thousand, one hundred thirty-eight
8. nine thousand, eight hundred seventy
9. 8,421   10. 4,385
11. 3,954   12. 5,736
13. 4,385   14. 9,870

Page 16
1. 8,810   2. 5,187
3. 700   4. 900
5. 900   6. 200
7. 6,000   8. 1,000
9. 7,000   10. 3,000
11. Check: 26

Page 17
1. 83   2. 58   3. 99
4. 67   5. 87   6. 49
7. 93   8. 66   9. 59
10. 48   11. 76   12. 97

Page 18
1. 55   2. 41   3. 10
4. 21   5. 47   6. 15
7. 32   8. 53   9. 31
10. 26   11. 68   12. 12

Page 19
1. 589   2. 894   3. 558
4. 467   5. 977   6. 742

Page 20
1. 447   2. 179   3. 356
4. 895   5. 699   6. 552
7. 748   8. 969   9. 773
10. 496   11. 949   12. 297
13. 664   14. 585   15. 794
16. 476

Page 21
1.
$$516$$
$$+ 349$$
$$500 + 300 = 800$$
$$10 + 40 = 50$$
$$6 + 9 = + 15$$
$$865$$

2.
$$399$$
$$+ 174$$
$$300 + 100 = 400$$
$$90 + 70 = 160$$
$$9 + 4 = + 13$$
$$573$$

3.
$$472$$
$$+ 225$$
$$400 + 200 = 600$$
$$70 + 20 = 90$$
$$2 + 5 = + 7$$
$$697$$

4.
$$534$$
$$+ 177$$
$$500 + 100 = 600$$
$$30 + 70 = 100$$
$$4 + 7 = + 11$$
$$711$$

5.
$$290$$
$$+ 636$$
$$200 + 600 = 800$$
$$90 + 30 = 120$$
$$0 + 6 = + 6$$
$$926$$

Page 21 (continued)
6.
$$198$$
$$+ 184$$
$$100 + 100 = 200$$
$$90 + 80 = 170$$
$$8 + 4 = + 12$$
$$382$$

7.
$$427$$
$$+ 296$$
$$400 + 200 = 600$$
$$20 + 90 = 110$$
$$7 + 6 = + 13$$
$$723$$

8.
$$688$$
$$+ 263$$
$$600 + 200 = 800$$
$$80 + 60 = 140$$
$$8 + 3 = + 11$$
$$951$$

Page 22
1. 911   2. 645   3. 791
4. 783   5. 421   6. 505
7. 832   8. 512   9. 932
10. 820   11. 700   12. 657

Page 23
1. 152   2. 423   3. 305
4. 121   5. 211   6. 446

Page 24
1. 714   2. 352   3. 824
4. 513   5. 261   6. 562
7. 442   8. 104   9. 137
10. 318   11. 331   12. 521
13. 705   14. 374   15. 429
16. 680

Page 25
1. 184   2. 208   3. 364
4. 148   5. 59   6. 289

Page 26
1. 288   2. 452   3. 696
4. 117   5. 228   6. 176
7. 245   8. 87   9. 689
10. 55   11. 148   12. 325

Page 27
1. 283   2. 175   3. 443
4. 246   5. 185   6. 19
7. 569   8. 657   9. 335
10. 149   11. 298   12. 72

Page 28
1. 350   2. 468   3. 279
4. 176   5. 356   6. 123
7. 286   8. 98   9. 293
10. 437   11. 89   12. 269
13. 122   14. 687   15. 162
16. 361

Page 29
1. 20   2. 17   3. 25
4. 50   5. 69   6. 185
7. 136   8. 143   9. 249
10. 513   11. 721   12. 800
13. 170   14. 226   15. 718
16. 959

Page 30
1. 161   2. 519   3. 790
4. 964   5. 152   6. 773
7. 625   8. 870

Page 31
1. 5,286   2. 3,737   3. 9,383
4. 7,820   5. 6,659   6. 4,745
7. 1,815   8. 4,006   9. 2,897
10. 7,589 11. 5,553 12. 6,738
13. 6,221 14. 3,426 15. 4,113
16. 9,805

Page 32
1. 6,511   2. 1,326   3. 4,484
4. 5,073   5. 9,262   6. 7,314
7. 4,939   8. 1,992   9. 1,121
10. 5,470 11. 3,442 12. 4,117
13. 3,478 14. 2,779 15. 7,454
16. 2,909

Page 33
1.
$$423$$ $$400$$
$$+ 271$$ $$+ 200$$
$$694$$ $$600$$

2.
$$190$$ $$100$$
$$+ 724$$ $$+ 700$$
$$914$$ $$800$$

3.
$$2,385$$ $$2,000$$
$$+ 612$$ $$+ 600$$
$$2,997$$ $$2,600$$

4.
$$8,732$$ $$8,000$$
$$+ 958$$ $$+ 900$$
$$9,690$$ $$8,900$$

5.
$$3,361$$ $$3,000$$
$$+4,518$$ $$+ 4,000$$
$$7,879$$ $$7,000$$

6.
$$2,112$$ $$2,000$$
$$+1,308$$ $$+1,000$$
$$3,420$$ $$3,000$$

Page 34
1.
$$872$$ $$800$$
$$- 661$$ $$-600$$
$$211$$ $$200$$

2.
$$925$$ $$900$$
$$- 629$$ $$-600$$
$$296$$ $$300$$

3.
$$6,734$$ $$6,000$$
$$- 322$$ $$- 300$$
$$6,412$$ $$5,700$$

4.
$$1,283$$ $$1,000$$
$$- 564$$ $$- 500$$
$$719$$ $$500$$

5.
$$4,826$$ $$4,000$$
$$-1,711$$ $$-1,000$$
$$3,115$$ $$3,000$$

6.
$$9,382$$ $$9,000$$
$$-7,449$$ $$-7,000$$
$$1,933$$ $$2,000$$

Answers

Page 35

1.
```
  436      400
+ 251    + 300
-----    -----
  687      700
```

2.
```
  166      200
+ 108    + 100
-----    -----
  274      300
```

3.
```
3,524    3,500
+ 367    + 400
-----    -----
3,891    3,900
```

4.
```
7,539    7,500
+ 616    + 600
-----    -----
8,155    8,100
```

5.
```
2,345    2,300
+2,354   +2,400
-----    -----
4,699    4,700
```

6.
```
4,181    4,200
+1,423   +1,400
-----    -----
5,604    5,600
```

Page 36

1.
```
  878      900
- 223    - 200
-----    -----
  655      700
```

2.
```
  795      800
- 519    - 500
-----    -----
  276      300
```

3.
```
6,428    6,400
-  411   -  400
-----    -----
6,017    6,000
```

4.
```
4,493    4,500
-  897   -  900
-----    -----
3,596    3,600
```

5.
```
8,781    8,800
-6,447   -6,400
-----    -----
2,334    2,400
```

6.
```
7,064    7,100
-1,815   -1,800
-----    -----
5,249    5,300
```

Page 37
1. 548   2. 8,804   3. 107

Page 38
1. 349   2. 623   3. 297

Page 39
1. 75   2. 111   3. 22
4. 39   5. 678   6. 931
7. 305   8. 294   9. 1,794
10. 5,600   11. 3,061   12. 6,609
13. 8,959   14. 7,012   15. 631
16. 1,327

Page 40

1.
```
  531      500      500
+ 324    + 300    + 300
-----    -----    -----
  855      800      800
```

2.
```
1,249    1,000    1,200
+ 217    + 200    + 200
-----    -----    -----
1,466    1,200    1,400
```

3.
```
  352      300      400
- 144    - 100    - 100
-----    -----    -----
  208      200      300
```

4.
```
4,671    4,000    4,700
- 728    - 700    - 700
-----    -----    -----
3,943    3,300    4,000
```

Page 41
1. 4   2. 12
3. 24   4. 16

Page 42
1. 10   2. 8
3. 5   4. 4

Page 43

Page 44
1. 8   2. 12   3. 4
4. 14   5. 6

Page 45
1. 15   2. 27   3. 21
4. 24   5. 40

Page 46
1. 20   2. 5   3. 35
4. 30   5. 10   6. 45
7. 25   8. 40   9. 50
10. 15

Page 47
1. 6   2. 0   3. 3
4. 0   5. 10   6. 0
7. 5   8. 0   9. 1
10. 0   11. 9   12. 0
13. 7   14. 0   15. 8
16. 0   17. 2   18. 0

Page 48
1. 28   2. 30   3. 48
4. 36   5. 60

Page 49
1. 10   2. 32   3. 100
4. 27   5. 35   6. 6
7. 30   8. 0   9. 12
10. 49   11. 54   12. 25
13. 16   14. 36   15. 21
16. 0   17. 64   18. 2

Page 50
1. 4   2. 35   3. 24
4. 12   5. 45   6. 20
7. 36   8. 0   9. 8
10. 81   11. 28   12. 15
13. 80   14. 0   15. 36
16. 30   17. 16   18. 16
19. 21   20. 72   21. 8
22. 1   23. 18   24. 45
25. 20   26. 40   27. 0
28. 18   29. 50   30. 9

Page 51
1. 6   2. 10   3. 4

Page 52
1. 6   2. 4
3. 2   4. 8

Page 53
1. 3   2. 5
3. 9   4. 6

Page 54
1. 6   2. 4   3. 5
4. 9   5. 2

Page 55
1. 8   2. 3   3. 10
4. 7   5. 7   6. 2
7. 7   8. 8   9. 8
10. 6   11. 9   12. 6
13. 9   14. 3   15. 7
16. 3   17. 4   18. 10

Page 56
1. 4   2. 10   3. 2
4. 9   5. 8   6. 5
7. 9   8. 7   9. 6
10. 9   11. 4   12. 3
13. 3   14. 5   15. 4
16. 6   17. 8   18. 8
19. 3   20. 10   21. 9
22. 7   23. 9   24. 7
25. 9   26. 2   27. 10
28. 5   29. 8   30. 4

Page 57
1. 1, 2, 4
2. 1, 2, 3, 6
3. 1, 3, 9
4. 1, 2, 3, 4, 6, 12
5. 1, 3, 5, 15
6. 1, 2, 4, 8, 16
7. 1, 2, 3, 6, 9, 18

Page 58

Page 59
1. 50, 40, 15, 20
2. 18

Page 60
1. 6, 2   2. 8

Page 61
1. 15   2. 72   3. 24
4. 5   5. 0   6. 20
7. 64   8. 9   9. 45
10. 16   11. 63   12. 28
13. 36   14. 60   15. 0
16. 48   17. 81   18. 18
19. 4   20. 6   21. 5
22. 7   23. 1   24. 2
25. 9   26. 7   27. 10
28. 3   29. 6   30. 3
31. 5   32. 2   33. 4
34. 8   35. 3   36. 7

Page 62
1. $5 \times 2 = 10$ 2. $6 \times 3 = 18$
  $2 \times 5 = 10$ $3 \times 6 = 18$
  $10 \div 5 = 2$ $18 \div 6 = 3$
  $10 \div 2 = 5$ $18 \div 3 = 6$

3. $4 \times 7 = 28$ 4. $3 \times 10 = 30$
  $7 \times 4 = 28$ $10 \times 3 = 30$
  $28 \div 4 = 7$ $30 \div 3 = 10$
  $28 \div 7 = 4$ $30 \div 10 = 3$

Page 63
1. $\frac{1}{2}$ 2. $\frac{3}{4}$ 3. $\frac{2}{3}$
4. $\frac{2}{5}$ 5. $\frac{3}{8}$ 6. $\frac{5}{6}$

Page 64

Page 65
1. $\frac{2}{3}$ 2. $\frac{5}{6}$ 3. $\frac{1}{4}$
4. $\frac{4}{7}$ 5. $\frac{6}{8}$ 6. $\frac{1}{10}$
7. $\frac{6}{9}$ 8. $\frac{3}{5}$

Page 66

Answers

Page 67
1. $\frac{4}{8}$ 2. $\frac{1}{5}$ 3. $\frac{7}{9}$
4. $\frac{2}{6}$ 5. $\frac{6}{10}$ 6. $\frac{3}{7}$

Page 68
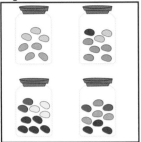

Page 69
1. $\frac{3}{7}$ 2. $\frac{5}{7}$ 3. $\frac{2}{3}$
4. $\frac{2}{4}$ 5. $\frac{1}{3}$ 6. $\frac{3}{4}$

Page 70
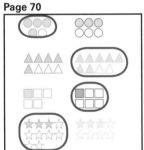

Page 71
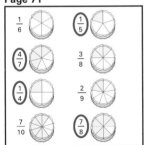

Page 72
1. >   2. >   3. <
4. =   5. <   6. >
7. <   8. <   9. >
10. > 11. > 12. =

Page 73
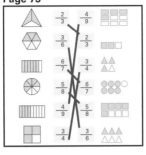

Page 74
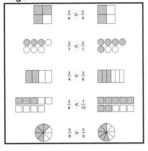

Page 75
1. 2, 5   2. 5, 13
3. 3, 8   4. 4, 10

Page 76
1. 3, 8   2. 1, 3   3. 5, 13
4. 2, 5   5. 4, 11 6. 6, 15

Page 77
1. inch   2. inch   3. foot
4. foot   5. yard

Page 78
1. centimeter
2. meter
3. centimeter
4. meter
5. meter
6. centimeter

Page 79
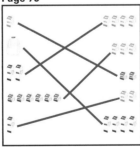

Page 80
1. gallon 2. cup
3. pint   4. gallon
5. cup   6. quart
7. gallon 8. pint

Page 81

Page 82
1. milliliter 2. liter
3. milliliter 4. milliliter
5. liter   6. milliliter
7. liter   8. liter

Page 83

Page 84
1. ounce   2. pound
3. ounce   4. pound
5. pound   6. ounce
7. ounce   8. pound

Page 85

Page 86
1. gram   2. kilogram
3. gram   4. gram
5. kilogram   6. gram
7. gram   8. kilogram

Page 87
1. 68, 20   2. 41, 5
3. 50, 10   4. 95, 35
5. 32, 0   6. 77, 25

Page 88

Page 89
1. 4, 10   2. 2, 5
3. 3, 8   4. 6, 15

Page 90
1. pound   2. gallon
3. gram   4. yard
5. quart   6. gallon
7. milliliter 8. meter

Page 91
1. <   2. >   3. =
4. >   5. =   6. <
7. >   8. <   9. >
10. = 11. < 12. >

Page 92
1. meter   2. degrees
3. gram   4. cup
5. pound   6. centimeter
7. gallon 8. inch

Page 93
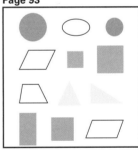

Page 94

	Number of vertices	Number of sides
	3	3
	4	4
	3	3
	6	6
	4	4

121

Answers

Page 95
1. 23
2. 22
3. 40
4. 27

Page 96
1. 15
2. 16
3. 12
4. 30
5. 54
6. 25

Page 97

Page 98

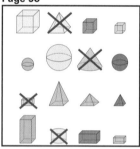

Page 99

	Number of vertices	Number of edges	Number of faces
	8	12	6
	5	8	5
	8	12	6
	4	6	4

Page 100

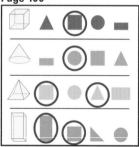

Page 101

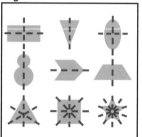

Page 102

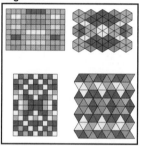

Page 103
1. fllp
2. turn
3. slide
4. flip
5. turn
6. slide
7. flip
8. turn

Page 104

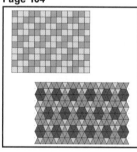

Page 105

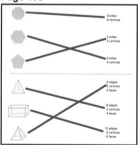

8 sides
8 vertices

5 sides
5 vertices

6 sides
6 vertices

8 edges
5 vertices
5 faces

6 edges
4 vertices
4 faces

12 edges
8 vertices
6 faces

Page 106
1. 32, 60
2. A 3. D 4. X
5. slide 6. turn 7. flip

Page 107
1. 10:02
2. 6:18
3. 2:44
4. 9:51
5. 11:27
6. 3:33

Page 108

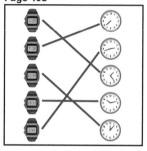

Page 109

Page 110
1. 4, 41
2. 2, 4
3. 2, 33
4. 3, 47

Page 111
1. 5, 0
2. 7, 30
3. 33, 45
4. 3, 45
5. 11, 15
6. 41, 40

Page 112
1. 9
2. 10
3. 8
4. 6
5. 7
6. 8

Fastest time per mile:

Page 113
$ 198.75

Page 114
1. $ 0.07
2. $ 1.05
3. $ 1.70
4. $ 3.06

Page 115

		GUEST CHECK			
Date	Table	Guests	Server		000903
4	Galaxy Burgers				$20.00
2	Sunburst Salads				$20.00
1	Freaky Fries				$2.00
3	Milky Way Milkshakes				$9.00
				Total	$51.00

		GUEST CHECK			
Date	Table	Guests	Server		000904
3	Pluto Burgers				$21.00
5	Black Hole Burgers				$45.00
2	Milky Way Milkshakes				$6.00
4	Mars Waters				$4.00
				Total	$76.00

Page 115 (continued)

		GUEST CHECK			
Date	Table	Guests	Server		000905
4	Galaxy Burgers				$20.00
9	Pluto Burgers				$63.00
3	Sunburst Salads				$30.00
6	Freaky Fries				$12.00
5	Mars Waters				$5.00
				Total	$130.00

		GUEST CHECK			
Date	Table	Guests	Server		000906
2	Pluto Burgers				$14.00
8	Black Hole Burgers				$72.00
2	Sunburst Salads				$20.00
5	Freaky Fries				$10.00
4	Milky Way Milkshakes				$12.00
				Total	$128.00

Page 116
1. $6.00
2. $2.25
3. $1.00
4. $5.00
5. $2.00
6. $2.00
7. $4.25
8. $3.00

Lowest price for 1 marble:

Page 117
1. 2, 15
2. 5:15
3. $45.00
4. 3 hours
5. $56.00

Page 118
1. 9:17, 12:51, 3, 34
2. 11:34, 4:43, 5, 9
3.

 $12.00

4. $64.00
5. $2.50